FESTIVE FARE

Lite

Menus

for

Playful

Days . . .

Ten percent of the net proceeds from this book benefits St. Jude Children's Research Hospital, Memphis, Tennessee.

TRADERY
H·O·U·S·E

Library of Congress Card Catalog Number: 95-60043
ISBN 1-879958-26-0

For additional copies, use the order form in the back of the book, or call The Wimmer Companies, Inc., 1-800-727-1034.

Printed in the USA by

WIMMER
The Wimmer Companies, Inc.
Memphis • Dallas

Table of Contents

Acknowledgments

. . . .

Special thanks to:

Lauren Swann, MS, RD, of Concept Nutrition, Inc., Bensalem, PA, for the recipe and menu development and the nutritional analysis and food hints. Lauren has more than 13 years of professional experience, with expertise in food marketing, labeling regulations, public relations, and community education.

Isabelle Hanson, Birmingham, AL, for writing the introduction and an essay on horseback riding.

The other talented writers from throughout the country for their memorable words.

Pashur House, Memphis, TN, for the cover design and other artwork found throughout the cookbook.

Introduction

Festive Fare may look like a cookbook. Actually, it is a guide to memory-making. What is the essence of a memorable occasion? Wonderful food, enlivening fun, enjoyable people, and interesting places. This "cookbook" does indeed offer delicious, simple recipes, but it goes way beyond a list of ingredients and procedures.

In *Festive Fare*, we present special warm-weather times—holidays, activities, and life transitions—as frameworks for creating memories. Writers from around the country highlight events in their own lives, sharing their feelings and images, from such occasions as Mother's Day to horseback riding to tailgating.

A health-conscious menu follows each activity, paying particular attention to budget and ease of preparation. What, for example, do you serve after a wild-and-wet canoe trip? We think the perfect Tipover Picnic includes Deep Sea Lobster Salad and Peachy Blueberry Delight. And for that back-to-school bash? A fiesta, of course, with Party Nachos, Light 'n' Spicy Beef Strips, and Tart 'n' Tangy Punch. Many of the book's recipes call for the willing contribution of little hands. Including children in the preparations is the perfect way to begin a family event.

The book also offers a big plus—numerous helpful tips (such as the one just given) on how to make your outing with family and friends truly a memory. These thoughtful tidbits offer a fun, organized approach to planning—helping you key in on particular destinations, suggesting experience-enhancing books, listing useful equipment, describing relationship-building activities, and more.

This entertaining and useful guidebook recognizes that in our hurry-up lifestyles, we often don't take enough time to "stop and smell the roses"—let alone enjoy a meal with family and friends. *Festive Fare* is designed to show you how to turn those "food and fun" occasions into small treasures you weave through your calendar of days. You've opened *Festive Fare*, so you're on your way. Here's to many memories in the making....

Mother's Day

Holding Court on a Porch Swing

It isn't very often that I get the opportunity or luxury to reflect back on my childhood memories. When I do, there are few memories that top Mother's Day celebrations at the park near our house.

The annual festivities began by sneaking out of church early so we could carry out our plans to divide and conquer the park. For many years we practiced this ritual to snag our favorite place—the spot by the pond with the swing.

This special place held what seemed like hundreds of large oak trees shading the sun, so that it displayed its rays in a mottled pattern on the park floor. It was equipped with a sturdy grill, picnic table, and a nicely weathered porch swing chained around a hardy limb hanging near the pond's edge. The pond was not very big, but it had an island in the center for the swans and mallards. They lazily swam by, demanding breadcrumbs as fee for our intrusion.

After unpacking the car, I spread out the gastronomic delights while my father took on the manly duty of preparing the grill. The table was adorned with a portable radio and a bouquet of flowers with high-flying balloons wishing her "Happy Mother's Day." Mom's favorite foods—mounds of corkscrew pasta salad, homemade hamburgers, baked beans floating in brown sugar, deviled eggs sprinkled with paprika, and plenty of Fritos—found their way to the table as well. (I think what Mom enjoyed most was that for one day there was at least one meal in which she was not conductor of the family symphony.)

After the feast, Mom proceeded to make her nest down by the pond, while my brothers threw a Frisbee or tossed the football. She ceremoniously dusted off an old, handmade family quilt and strategically placed it in the sun. Then she basked in the spring sunshine like a lazy cat, with the Sunday paper in a circle around her.

In reflecting back to those days in the park, I have now concluded that if the truth be known, this isn't just a "family spot." It is her spot, on her special day with her family around her. It is her time to be sentimental and mushy. It is her prerogative to be quiet and finish her current romance novel or to hold court on the old porch swing near the pond. (Court was held with each child, never rushing but taking time to listen to details of our lives.)

No matter how far away I go or how old I get, I will never forget those special Mother's Days. And when the time comes for family traditions to pass from one generation to the next, I want to be just like Mom—holding court on a porch swing in the park.

Lori Loper
Memphis, TN

PLAN A SURPRISE DAY FOR YOUR MOTHER. Tell her how to dress and what time to be ready and nothing else. Take her somewhere she's never been before and do something she's never done (bungee jumping may not be a good idea). Some suggestions: lunch and antique shopping in a nearby town; a nature walk with a packed lunch for the trail; a trip to your office with a picnic at your desk— explain what you do and let her know your success has a lot to do with how she reared you.

COME HOME FOR THE WEEKEND without letting your mother know— if fact, tell her the opposite and then surprise her. If there's a sibling who financially can't make it home, help them out, if possible; your mother will be thrilled that they are there and that you were thoughtful enough to help. It will make her day that much more special.

If you don't SEND FLOWERS ON MOTHER'S DAY, try it this year. Pick up a bunch at your local florist or at the grocery store. Even a few attractive stems with greenery will make Mom feel important. If you are distant, have them delivered the day before and follow up with a phone call. If your mother is deceased, place flowers on the gravesite and/or give a donation to her favorite charity in her memory. Then spend the day doing something she would have enjoyed.

Menu for Mom

Stuffed Cherry Tomatoes

❦ ❦ ❦

Marinated Vegetables
Vinaigrette Chicken
Chillin' Out Spaghetti

❦ ❦ ❦

Apricot Chiffon Pie
Summertime Spritzer

❦ ❦ ❦

Stuffed Cherry Tomatoes

20 cherry tomatoes
¼ cup nonfat cottage cheese
¼ cup minced onion
1 tablespoon black pepper

Thinly slice tops off tomatoes. Scoop out pulp. Mix pulp with cottage cheese, onion, and black pepper. Fill tomatoes with mixture before serving.

Yield: 20 appetizers

Nutrients per 3 tomatoes:

Calories 34 Fat 0 g Carbohydrate 6 g Protein 3 g Sodium 74 mg Cholesterol 2 mg

Marinated Vegetables

2 cups cauliflower flowerets
2 cups broccoli flowerets
1 cup carrot slices
2 cups balsamic vinegar
1 teaspoon black pepper
1 teaspoon garlic powder
1 teaspoon onion powder

Mix vegetables together; set aside. Combine vinegar and spices; pour over vegetables. Marinade vegetables in refrigerator overnight.

Yield: 8 servings

Nutrients per serving:

Calories 18 Fat 0 g Carbohydrate 4 g Protein 2 g Sodium 11 mg Cholesterol 0 mg

Make low-fat meals appealing with menus that include foods of different colors, textures, and shapes.

Vinaigrette Chicken

1½ pounds cooked, skinned
    chicken breast, diced
1 cup sliced green onion
2 cups cooked corn
2 cups shredded red
    cabbage
2 cups balsamic vinegar
2 tablespoons lemon juice
2 teaspoons black pepper

*Combine chicken and vegetables;
set aside. Mix vinegar, lemon
juice, and black pepper together;
stir into chicken vegetable mixture. Chill before serving.*

Yield: 8 servings

Nutrients per serving:

Calories 180 Fat 3 g Carbohydrate 12 g Protein 28 g Sodium 352 mg Cholesterol 73 mg

Chillin' Out Spaghetti

8 ounces spaghetti
2 tablespoons olive oil
2 tablespoons balsamic
    vinegar
2 tablespoons minced garlic
¼ cup parsley
1 cup broccoli flowerets

*Break spaghetti in half, and cook
per package directions; drain
and cool. Mix oil, vinegar, garlic,
and parsley together; set aside.
Combine spaghetti and broccoli
in large bowl. Pour seasoned
liquid mixture over spaghetti,
and toss to mix well. Serve chilled
or at room temperature.*

Yield: 8 servings

Nutrients per serving:

Calories 83 Fat 4 g Carbohydrate 11 g Protein 2 g Sodium 3 mg Cholesterol 0 mg

Apricot Chiffon Pie

2 small packages sugar-free
  pudding mix
2 cups light whipped
  topping
2 cups chopped apricots
2 (8-inch) graham cracker
  crusts, baked

*Prepare pudding as directed
using skim milk. Fold in whipped
topping and apricots. Pour into
crust; chill thoroughly before
serving.*

Yield: 12 servings

Nutrients per serving:

Calories 222 Fat 7 g Carbohydrate 32 g Protein 4 g Sodium 444 Cholesterol 0 mg

Summertime Spritzer

4 cups seltzer
4 cups orange juice
2 cups grape juice
 Orange rings (optional)

*Combine seltzer and juices; mix
well. Serve over ice. Garnish with
orange rings, if desired.*

Yield: 10 cups

Nutrients per 1 cup:

Calories 54 Fat 0 g Carbohydrate 14 g Protein 0 g Sodium 2 mg Cholesterol 0 mg

Wildflower Wonder

The Fifth Season

In grade school I learned there are four seasons: winter, spring, summer, fall. I also learned there are 12 months, and in a child's simple assumption of the fairness of life, I thought that divided quite neatly into three months per season. That was before I moved to Texas as a college student and discovered that in Central Texas, at least, the seasons are far from equitable. Summer, for instance, begins in May and extends its hot, baking hand over life as we know it through late September. Winter is an icy-fingered guerrilla, striking from the wings of random cold fronts, only to surrender its grip on people and land within a week. Spring and fall are states of mind.

With the seasons observing such ragged time boundaries, it's no surprise that my friends and I observe a fifth season—wildflower weather—which blossoms on the fringe of summer in Central Texas. It has its heralds as faithful as any Pennsylvanian groundhog: the first clump of purplish bluebonnets in an unmown yard, heavy spring rains that rarely linger, a toasty afternoon sun whose rays do not yet blister and burn. It calls us to Saturday drives along the highways and meandering rural lanes of neighboring counties, where the natural primary colors of bluish bluebonnets, scarlet Indian paintbrush, and canary yellow coreopsis soften hard scrabble road shoulders and spatter fields doomed to yellow and brown in the oven of July and August.

Wildflower weather is perfect for picnicking—well, perfect if one can calmly lay out a luncheon spread while the same breezes that make the bluebonnets bob and sway, pick up loose paper napkins, half-emptied potato chip bags, and unfastened tablecloth corners and threaten to blow them across the county line. Practice makes perfect, and over several years of leading caravans of wildflowering friends, we've gotten the hang of anchoring wind-friendly items with pickle jars, trays of brownies, and Tupperware containers brimming with potato salad.

Our picnics offer simple fare, but simple are the joys of wildflower weather: warm sun, breezes heavy with the lavender musk of bluebonnet, blankets spread upon the ground, unpressured talks with good friends. Calendars and cluttered schedules don't enter the picture here. Why should they, when they don't recognize this fifth season of the year?

Carl Hoover
Waco, Texas

To obtain more information about WHAT TYPES OF WILDFLOWERS ARE BLOOMING, where they are blooming, and when they have their peak season, contact the National Wildflower Research Center at (512) 832-4059, ext. 4.

 IF YOU CAN'T GO TO THE WILDFLOWERS, then bring them to you. Grow a wildflower garden in your own backyard. Be careful in your seed selection because seeds sold in bulk as mixed wildflowers may contain an abundance of wild grass seeds. Ask your local nursery to recommend seeds that would do well in your area, and the time of year to plant them. Be patient because wildflowers take a while to establish from seeds.

SOME WILDFLOWERS ARE PROTECTED by state and federal regulations, so do not pick or dig up wildflowers without permission or knowledge of what you are allowed to do. Many areas have designated digs, so check with your local botanic gardens to get the information you need.

D I N E   A M O N G   T H E   F L O W E R S

Marinated Harvest
Asparagus Pasta Salad
Lighter Antipasto

❦ ❦ ❦

Grilled Eggplant Sandwiches

❦ ❦ ❦

Grape-Tasting Apples
Hearty Punch

❦ ❦ ❦

Marinated Harvest

2 cups broccoli flowerets
2 cups mini carrots
1 cucumber, sliced
1 (8-ounce) bottle nonfat
   dressing

Combine vegetables. Pour dressing over vegetables, cover, and marinate several hours or overnight.

Yield: 8 servings

Nutrients per serving:

Calories 49 g Fat 1 g Carbohydrate 9 g Protein 3 g Sodium 278 mg Cholesterol 0 mg

Asparagus Pasta Salad

12 ounces ziti, cooked and
   drained
2 cups asparagus, cut in
   1-inch pieces
¼ cup diced yellow bell
   pepper
¼ cup diced onion
¼ cup nonfat Italian
   dressing
1 teaspoon black pepper

Combine ziti, asparagus, bell pepper, and onion. Mix well. Add dressing and black pepper. Toss to moisten all ingredients. Chill before serving.

Yield: 6 servings

Nutrients per serving

Calories 233 Fat 2 g Carbohydrate 45 g Protein 8 g Sodium 145 mg Cholesterol 0 mg

Lighter Antipasto

2 tomatoes, cut into wedges
1 zucchini squash, cut into sticks
1 pound turkey kielbasa, cut into 1-inch chunks
1 carrot, cut into sticks
Nonfat Italian dressing (optional)

Arrange all ingredients in above order on serving tray. Serve with nonfat Italian dressing, if desired.

Yield: 6 servings

Nutrients per serving:

Calories 152 g Fat 10 g Carbohydrate 14 g Protein 11 g Sodium 635 mg Cholesterol 35 mg

Grilled Eggplant Sandwiches

1 large eggplant
1 cup nonfat red wine and vinegar dressing
1 teaspoon basil
¼ teaspoon black pepper
½ teaspoon parsley
5 (5-inch) submarine rolls

Peel eggplant; cut into ½-inch slices. Mix dressing with spices, and pour over eggplant slices in shallow dish. Allow to marinate 1 hour or longer. Grill for approximately 8 minutes or until tender. For each sandwich, layer two eggplant slices on a submarine roll.

Yield: 5 servings

Nutrients per serving:

Calories 229 g Fat 4 g Carbohydrate 36 g Protein 6 g Sodium 341 mg Cholesterol 0 mg

Grape-Tasting Apples

2 medium apples
Cinnamon
1½ cups grapes
5 tablespoons light whipped
   topping

*Peel apples, and cut into cubes.
Toss with cinnamon, and then
combine with grapes. Divide into
5 servings; top each with 1
tablespoon whipped topping.*

Yield: 5 servings

Nutrients per serving

Calories 50 g Fat 0 g Carbohydrate 12 g Protein 0 g Sodium 0 mg Cholesterol 0 mg

Hearty Punch

1 quart orange juice
1 quart grapefruit juice
1 quart grape juice
1 quart diet ginger ale
1 quart seltzer water

*Mix juices, soda, and seltzer
together in a large container.
Serve over ice.*

Yield: 26 (6-ounce) servings

Nutrients per serving:

Calories 71 g Fat 0 g Carbohydrate 18 g Protein 0 g Sodium 0 mg Cholesterol 0 mg

The very appearance of your meals adds to the satisfaction. Enjoy the bright colors of summertime foods.

Kite Flying

Dancing With the Clouds

Some people's heartstrings are found close to home. As a child, mine danced up into the sky and waltzed with the clouds. All I needed was a Gulf breeze and a kite.

The pewter skies of winter are easily forgotten with the coming of spring. When I was young, this was my favorite time of year, not because of blooming azaleas, rising temperatures, or the pilgrimage of tourists to my beachside community but because with the new season came strong winds perfect for kites.

On the first breezy day, my family always drove down to the beach. There we didn't have to worry about trees or power lines blocking the flight path. The spring of my seventh year, my parents bought me my very own red kite. My sister, Amy, got a blue one.

My father taught me the proper way to launch my new kite. He held it in his hands while I raced down the shoreline clutching its string. At just the right moment, he let go. Whoosh! Up into the sky it flew. I did it! My kite was off the ground. At the water's edge, I stopped running and stretched my neck back to watch my own private air show.

Inch by inch, I released the line like my dad told me. I could feel the kite's pulse surging through the string as it gained altitude.

Amy, who had flown kites before, guided her kite to do twists and turns, often nosediving it into a sand dune. But not me. I wanted to fly into the clouds that before had always seemed just out of my reach.

I stood still listening to the whip of the salty wind as it pulled my kite higher and farther out over the Gulf. I was so busy looking up that I didn't realize I was at the end of the string until it slipped from my grasp. I jumped, hoping to grab it, but it was too late. Helpless, I watched my kite grow smaller and smaller until it finally disappeared behind a white cloud.

I turned away in time to see my sister's kite crash into the ground yet again. At that moment, I smiled knowing that my kite was off dancing with the clouds. Since that day, I always anxiously await that first dance of spring.

Lisa Camino
Mary Esther, FL

19

BE CAUTIOUS WHEN FLYING KITES to make sure you are away from overhead power lines. Never fly kites in thunderstorms, and always make sure children are supervised.

 SOME OF THE BEST SOURCES FOR PURCHASING KITES are hobby shops and gift shops of museums and zoos. You'll usually find unique shapes and designs to soar toward the clouds.

 THE GIFT SHOP OF THE AIR AND SPACE MUSEUM at the Smithsonian Institute in Washington, D.C. sells a large variety of kites and sponsors a kite-flying contest on The Mall in the springtime. For more information, call (202) 357-2700.

B R E E Z Y D E L I G H T S

Zesty Spinach Dip
Corny Pepper Slaw

❦ ❦ ❦

Rice and Veggie Mix
Marinated Chicken Breast Sandwich

❦ ❦ ❦

Saucy Fruit Refresher
Summer's Eve Spritzer

❦ ❦ ❦

Zesty Spinach Dip

1 (10-ounce) package frozen chopped spinach
1 (8-ounce) container plain nonfat yogurt
1 (8-ounce) container nonfat sour cream
¼ cup chopped red onion
1 teaspoon garlic powder
⅛ teaspoon hot sauce

Cook spinach according to package directions; let cool. Combine yogurt, sour cream, onion, garlic powder, and hot sauce until well blended. Mix with spinach. Cover and chill. Serve with whole-grain crackers.

Yield: about 3 cups

Nutrients per 1 tablespoon:

Calories 8 g Fat 0 g Carbohydrate 1 g Protein 0 g Sodium 12 mg Cholesterol 0 mg

Corny Pepper Slaw

1 cup cooked corn
1 cup diced green bell pepper
1 cup diced red bell pepper
2 tablespoons chopped parsley
1 cup reduced-calorie creamy Italian dressing

Mix vegetable together; stir in Italian dressing just before serving.

Yield: 6 servings

Nutrients per serving:

Calories 102 Fat 7 g Carbohydrate 14 g Protein 0 g Sodium 335 mg Cholesterol 0 mg

Rice and Veggie Mix

2 cups broccoli flowerets
2 cups sliced celery
1 (8-ounce) bottle nonfat
  Italian dressing
1 cup cooked rice

*Combine broccoli and celery.
Pour dressing over mixture, and
marinate 1 hour or more. Serve
marinated vegetables over rice.*

Yield: 6 servings

Nutrients per serving:

Calories 67 Fat 0 g Carbohydrate 12 g Protein 3 g Sodium 818 mg Cholesterol 0 mg

Marinated Chicken Breast Sandwich

½ cup red wine vinegar
¼ cup lemon juice
1 tablespoon vegetable oil
1 teaspoon black pepper
½ teaspoon onion powder
3 boneless, skinless chicken
  breasts, split
6 kaiser rolls

*Combine first 5 ingredients; mix
well. Pour over chicken, and
allow to marinate in refrigerator
1 to 2 hours. Remove chicken
from mixture. Grill, steam, or
bake breasts. Serve on kaiser rolls.*

Yield: 6 servings

Nutrients per serving:

Calories 316 Fat 7 g Carbohydrate 30 g Protein 27 g Sodium 376 mg Cholesterol 73 mg

Saucy Fruit Refresher

1 cup nonfat vanilla yogurt
1 cup nonfat sour cream
½ cup strawberry fruit
   spread
2 large bananas
4 medium apples

Combine first 3 ingredients; chill.
Cut bananas and apples into
large chunks; serve with fruit
sauce as a topping or dip.

Yield: 8 servings

Nutrients per serving:

Calories 230 Fat 0 g Carbohydrate 52 g Protein 5 g Sodium 68 mg Cholesterol 0 mg

Summer's Eve Spritzer

4 cups cranberry juice
   cocktail
2 cups diet ginger ale
½ cup grape juice
½ cup seltzer water

Combine cranberry juice, ginger
ale, and grape juice; mix well.
Stir in seltzer water. Serve over
ice.

Yield: 9 (6-ounce) servings

Nutrients per serving:

Calories 80 Fat 0 g Carbohydrate 20 g Protein 0 g Sodium 0 mg Cholesterol 0 mg

Chilled foods are cool, refreshing, and palate cleansing for light eating.

Team Sports

PASHUR

Soccer: Like Life—A Kick in the Grass

For the past 15 years, soccer was more than just a sport to my family. It was the benchmark to measure the growth of our son and the evolution of our family. He was 6 years old when he played in his first soccer match. Getting him there was the real task, though, as at the last minute he stubbornly refused to leave the comfort of his home and favorite childhood blanket for the unfamiliar world of youth soccer competition. The photographs taken then—blue-and-white uniforms, $18 Adidas molded cleats, and almost all 22 players from both teams in the same frame going for the ball—elicit memories that seem sharper in focus than the photos themselves.

Events after that first match blur together; time seemingly has passed so quickly. Local soccer camps were replaced by those in distant states. Practices became more frequent; getting him to and from them was replaced with typical parents' worries about the driving habits of young adolescents. Soccer shoes became much more expensive, and specialized—different cleats for different field conditions were required by "serious" players. Teams that used to play in the community on Saturdays in the fall and spring became traveling teams playing entire weekends throughout the year from Florida to North Carolina to Texas. We've been to small Alabama and Mississippi communities that I would never guess had a soccer field. We've sweltered in the June heat of Dallas and shivered in the December cold of Memphis. But no one complained (too much) and our best friends (and travel companions) were other soccer families.

Our son is now 21 and a college junior. We have not seen him play soccer for more than a year, although he still actively competes in the sport, but distance and growing independence limit our involvement. Our memories are rich, however. A wall in our house holds photographs from the early soccer days and from more recent ones. The picture of a young boy with his first championship medal is next to one of a decidedly confident, mature young man who has just made the winning penalty kick.

Soccer presented the three of us with a common ground for involvement and contributed the framework for the development of our family. It is very common for us to relate our family life events to certain soccer events we all experienced. Certainly, our memories will be colored by these experiences for many years to come.

John Boker
Memphis, TN

Part of the REASON FOR YOUTH TO PARTICIPATE IN TEAM SPORTS is for the camaraderie of the experience. Add to that by entering the team in a tournament, especially one where the team members have to travel and spend more time together than just for a few hours a week.

 SUGGEST A CHILD VERSUS PARENT SOCCER MATCH at the beginning of the season so the parents and kids can all get to know one another. Have one at the end of the season too. You'll be impressed with how much you child has improved during the season. (By the way, only do this when they are under-12 bracket or younger. You can't begin to keep up with them after that.)

 IF YOUR KIDS ARE PAST LITTLE LEAGUE OR SOCCER PLAYING and you miss the activity, get involved. Many local younger teams desperately need coaches and assistants, so volunteer your time and talents.

S P O R T S   S U P P E R

Colorful Cheese Cubes
Tangy Carrot Sticks

🍎 🍎 🍎

Turkey-Stuffed Pitas
Cinnamon Fruit Salad

🍎 🍎 🍎

Banana Nutter Cookies
Sunshine Grape Punch

🍎 🍎 🍎

Colorful Cheese Cubes

2 ounces reduced-fat sharp Cheddar cheese
2 ounces reduced-fat Monterey Jack cheese
1 tablespoon paprika
2 tablespoons chopped chives

Cut cheeses into ½-inch cubes. Mix paprika and chives; toss cheese cubes in paprika-chive mixture.

Yield: about 24 cubes

Nutrients per 2 cubes (one of each type):

Calories 27 Fat 2 g Carbohydrate 0 g Protein 3 g Sodium 73 mg Cholesterol 6 mg

Tangy Carrot Sticks

1 cup reduced-calorie red wine and vinegar dressing
1 cup finely chopped green bell pepper
1 teaspoon black pepper
4 medium carrots, scraped

Combine dressing, bell pepper, and black pepper. Cut carrots into lengthwise quarters. Pour dressing mixture over carrots, and allow to marinate before serving.

Yield: 8 servings

Nutrients per serving:

Calories 65 Fat 5 g Carbohydrate 3 g Protein 0 g Sodium 315 mg Cholesterol 0 mg

Soccer is an endurance sport, so carbohydrates the day before are recommended—and no greasy food before the match. Drinking cold water before, during, and after the game is a must to replenish what the body loses. Bananas and oranges provide a good halftime snack.

Turkey-Stuffed Pitas

6 mini pita rounds
¼ cup mustard
6 turkey sandwich slices
6 tomato slices, halved

For each sandwich, cut mini rounds in half; then open. Spread inside of each half with 1 teaspoon mustard. Cut turkey slices into quarters. Fill each pita half with 2 quarter slices of turkey and 1 tomato slice half.

Yield: 12 sandwich "pockets"

Nutrients per pocket:

Calories 82 Fat 0 g Carbohydrate 16 g Protein 4 g Sodium 83 mg Cholesterol 5 mg

Cinnamon Fruit Salad

2 medium oranges
2 medium peaches
2 cups pineapple chunks
2 teaspoons cinnamon

Peel oranges and peaches; cut into chunks, and combine with pineapple. Toss fruit chunks with cinnamon.

Yield: 8 servings

Nutrients per serving:

Calories 75 Fat 0 g Carbohydrate 18 g Protein 1 g Sodium 0 mg Cholesterol 6 mg

Banana Nutter Cookies

1 small banana, mashed
¼ cup margarine
½ cup peanut butter
⅓ cup white sugar
⅓ cup brown sugar
1 egg
½ teaspoon vanilla extract
½ teaspoon baking soda
1 cup flour

Preheat oven to 325°. Cream together banana, margarine, and peanut butter. Add sugars and then remaining ingredients. Place dough by tablespoonfuls onto greased cookie sheets, and flatten with a fork. Bake for about 8 minutes.

Yield: 2 dozen cookies

Nutrients per cookie:

Calories 81 Fat 5 g Carbohydrate 7 g Protein 2 g Sodium 61 mg Cholesterol 6 mg

Sunshine Grape Punch

3 cups orange juice
1 cup lemon juice
2 cups ginger ale
1 cup grape juice
1 cup water

Combine all ingredients. Chill before serving.

Yield: 8 cups

Nutrients per 1 cup:

Calories 84 Fat 0 g Carbohydrate 22 g Protein 0 g Sodium 6 mg Cholesterol 0 mg

If you have a post-game picnic, remember to include finger foods, especially at outdoor activities. The fun always seems to keep them on the go. Cut vegetables and fruits into wedges and chunks, just the right size to prevent choking.

29

Memorial Day

PASHUR

Honoring the Past

When I grew up in a small coal mining town in southwest Virginia, Memorial Day was simply known as Decoration Day. I still recall gathering with my family and neighbors to make a long hike to a cemetery located on one of the many steep mountains in Buchanan County. The cemetery was established in the mid-1800's, and most families in the community had relatives buried there.

The cemetery had no caretaker, so upkeep fell upon the townspeople. Each family began preparations prior to the event: They purchased plastic flowers at the local five-and-dime store and then sharpened hoes, bush axes, and other tools. The night before, the smells of cornbread and fried chicken coming from the kitchens filled everyone with anticipation for the pending feast.

Early Decoration Day morning, families met at the base of the mountain. During the long walk, neighbors caught up on the latest gossip, and cousins who had not seen each other for a while laughed about their youthful antics. A few copperheads and black snakes always appeared during the hike, as well as box turtles that amused the youngsters.

As the cemetery came into view, voices seemed to soften to a whisper. Upon arrival, families separated to find the graves of their relatives. The cemetery had few visitors during the year, but it was a lively place on Decoration Day. Men and women used the tools to cut the heavy brush that grew the past summer and uprighted headstones that were overturned during the spring thaw. As they worked, they remembered stories of those they were honoring. The cemetery took on a new appearance as the sunlight reached through the tops of the trees. Colorful new flowers replaced the faded ones—even on the graves that had illegible markers of unclaimed loved ones.

With the cleanup and decorating complete, a preacher usually said a prayer and delivered a short sermon before lunch. Then families dug into their baskets for all the prepared goodies. After the meal, it was time to retreat from the mountain. Most folks paused at the entrance to take another look at the clean, newly decorated site. It was as if the act of honoring the past through hard work gave them an extra boost of energy to travel the path home.

It's been more than 20 years since I visited the cemetery. I doubt if I could even locate the mountain again if I tried. But on warm Memorial Days—I can find the tidy cemetery in my memory.

Kathy Still
Bristol Herald Courier
Norton, VA

GO TO A LOCAL CEMETERY. Pull some weeds, and place some flowers at a gravesite that looks neglected. Do a rubbing of the headstone, and research the name through public records. Attend to the gravesite throughout the year.

 SPEND THE MEMORIAL DAY WEEKEND in our Nation's Capital. A Presidential Wreath is laid annually at the Tomb of the Unknown Soldier in Arlington Cemetery. The President or Vice President usually performs this duty around mid-morning on Memorial Day. Later in the day, ceremonies are held at the Vietnam Memorial to honor the veterans of that war. There is plenty to see and do in Washington, D.C. for a long weekend, so have some fun besides taking the time to honor those who died for their country. For more information, call the Washington, D.C. Convention and Visitors Association: (202) 789-7000.

ATTEND A PARADE, as your community honors its heroes on this day. Invite some neighbors back for this festive supper.

M E M O R A B L E   M E N U

Cucumber Relish
Crunchy Coleslaw

❧ ❧ ❧

Backyard Turkey Burgers
Roasted Potato Surprise

❧ ❧ ❧

Fluffy Berry Pies
Berry Iced Tea

❧ ❧ ❧

Cucumber Relish

1 cucumber, chopped
¼ cup balsamic vinegar
¼ cup chopped onion
½ teaspoon black pepper
2 tablespoons minced red
   bell pepper

Combine all ingredients. Mix well. Use as a spread on hot dogs, hamburgers, and sandwiches.

Yield: about 1 cup

Nutrients per tablespoon:

Calories 3 Fat 0 g Carbohydrate 0 g Protein 1 g Sodium 0 mg Cholesterol 0 mg

Crunchy Coleslaw

1 cup shredded green
   cabbage
1 cup shredded red cabbage
½ cup chopped onion
1 cup grated carrot
¼ cup vinegar
1 teaspoon celery seed
1 cup nonfat mayonnaise

Mix vegetables and spices together until well combined. Add mayonnaise; mix well. Chill before serving.

Yield: 8 servings

Nutrients per serving:

Calories 38 Fat 0 g Carbohydrate 9 g Protein 0 g Sodium 405 mg Cholesterol 0 mg

Lighter whipped topping gives the "feeling" of indulgent desserts, but is surprisingly lower in calories.

Backyard Turkey Burgers

2 pounds ground turkey breast
2 tablespoons prepared horseradish
½ teaspoon black pepper
1 cup tomato sauce

Combine turkey with horseradish and pepper. Add tomato sauce; mix well. Shape into 8 patties. Broil or grill until well done.

Yield: 8 servings

Nutrients per serving:

Calories 180 Fat 3 g Carbohydrate 2 g Protein 26 g Sodium 52 mg Cholesterol 55 mg

Roasted Potato Surprise

8 medium potatoes
½ cup diet margarine
1 teaspoon black pepper
½ teaspoon red pepper
1 tablespoon chives

Scrub potatoes. Soften margarine; mix in spices and chives. Split each potato in half. Spread 1 tablespoon margarine mixture inside each potato. Close potatoes, and wrap in foil. Cook over hot charcoal until tender.

Yield: 8 servings

Nutrients per potato:

Calories 160 Fat 6 g Carbohydrate 23 g Protein 3 g Sodium 136 mg Cholesterol 0 mg

Fluffy Berry Pies

2 (4-serving) packages sugar-free fruit-flavored gelatin
1 cup raspberries
1 cup blueberries
1 cup thawed light whipped topping
12 individual graham cracker crusts

Prepare gelatin per package directions until partially set. Gently fold in fruit and whipped topping; spoon ½ cup mixture into each individual crust. Return to refrigerator, and chill until firm.

Yield: 12 pies

Nutrients per pie:

Calories 58 Fat 2 g Carbohydrate 4 g Protein 0 g Sodium 71 mg Cholesterol 0 mg

Berry Iced Tea

2 quarts water, divided
4 tea bags
2 cups cranberry juice cocktail
Lemon slices
Sugar or sweetener to taste

Bring 1 quart water to a boil; pour over tea bags in heat-resistant pitcher. Steep for 5 minutes; add 1 quart cold water and cranberry juice cocktail; stir well. Refrigerate until thoroughly chilled; serve over ice. Garnish with lemon slices, and sweeten to taste, if desired.

Yield: 10 cups

Nutrients per (1 cup) serving:

Calories 33 Fat 0 g Carbohydrate 8 g Protein 0 g Sodium 0 mg Cholesterol 0 mg

Tennis

If You Can't Lick 'Em...Maybe Your Partner Can

She stands at the net in utter defiance: feet shoulder-width apart, racket firmly in hand, unblinking eyes staring holes through the opposition. She wears solids, not frivolous prints. Her hair is short or else pulled back in a no-non-sense ponytail. Her visor is firmly in place. And she got that tan on the courts, not in some coconut-scented salon with parrots painted on the front window. You'd better not cross her. She is Tournament Woman.

I first encountered Tournament Woman when a good friend offered to be my doubles partner in a local charity tournament. "It would be fun," she said. And then she mumbled something about tournament rules and how we'd have to compete at the level of the highest-ranking member of our team. "I guess I'm, oh, about a 4.0 player," she said with a shrug. "Let's just give that level a try." (Translation: *"I could give Navratilova a run for her money, and so could everybody else we'll be playing, so if you own a rabbit's foot, you might want to bring it."*)

I eagerly anticipated my first serious athletic competition. I put all the essentials in my tennis bag: sunscreen, gum, moisturizer, lip balm, hairbrush, hair spray...you get the picture. Then I dressed in a colorful ensemble of lovely pastels. It was sort of a theatrical experience, like putting on a costume to play a nifty role for a few hours.

Only when I stepped onto the court did I realize that I was actually expected to *hit the ball.* And it would be coming at me *really really fast.* My jaw dropped to my knees as I watched Tournament Woman warming up with her partner. Nothing escaped her reach. She returned every shot calmly, deliberately, decisively. Not a single "oops" did she utter. Not once did she giggle as a misplaced lob sailed over the fence and bounced off the hood of a Corvette.

I won't go into the details of that match. Let's just say it didn't take Tournament Woman long to figure out that she should hit everything to me. Fortunately, however, my partner kept up a ceaseless barrage of praise for the points I actually made and encouragement after the many that I lost. In the end, we didn't win the match, but we didn't let Tournament Woman throttle us either. The moral of this story: It's not whether you win or lose; it's whether you can talk an awesome player into being your partner. And it never hurts to have a nice warm-up jacket that complements your tennis skirt.

Mattie Lee
Vestavia, AL

In New Braunfels, Texas, the John Newcombe Tennis Ranch offers TENNIS ACADEMIES. For more information, call (210) 625-9105.

 For details on TENNIS CAMPS, CLINICS, AND TENNIS PROGRAMS under the direction of Roy Barth, contact Kiawah Island Resort, East Beach Tennis Center, 12 Kiawah Beach Drive, Kiawah Island, SC 29455; or call (803) 768-2121.

Most communities have COMMUNITY CENTERS WITH TENNIS COURTS. Get involved just for good exercise or take lessons to improve your skills. Many centers sponsor leagues—daytime and evening. Playing in league competition at your skill level provides a great opportunity to meet people in the community.

G A M E ,   S E T ,   M A T C H ,   L U N C H

Chunky Pepper Salsa
Squash Salad
Tangy Macaroni Salad

❦ ❦ ❦

Turkey Loaf Sandwiches

❦ ❦ ❦

Tropical Citrus Mix
High-Energy Sparkler

❦ ❦ ❦

Chunky Pepper Salsa

2 medium tomatoes, chopped
1 medium-size green bell pepper, chopped
½ cup chopped onion
1 tablespoon red wine vinegar
1 tablespoon oregano
1 tablespoon cumin powder

Combine all ingredients, and mix well. Chill salsa thoroughly. Serve with oil-free tortilla chips.

Yield: 1½ cups

Nutrients per ¼-cup serving:

Calories 16 Fat 0 g Carbohydrate 3 g Protein 0 g Sodium 3 mg Cholesterol 0 mg

Squash Salad

1 medium yellow squash, sliced
1 medium zucchini squash, sliced
¼ cup sliced onion
½ teaspoon basil
½ teaspoon tarragon
⅔ cup white wine vinegar

Combine yellow squash, zucchini, and onion; sprinkle with herbs. Toss mixture with vinegar.

Yield: 8 (½-cup) servings

Nutrients per serving:

Calories 18 Fat 0 g Carbohydrate 3 g Protein 0 g Sodium 1 mg Cholesterol 0 mg

Tangy Macaroni Salad

2 cups cooked elbow
  macaroni
1 cup sliced celery
½ cup nonfat plain yogurt
¼ cup green onion slices
1 tablespoon Dijon mustard

Combine all ingredients, and mix well. Chill salad before serving.

Yield: 10 (½-cup) servings

Nutrients per serving:

Calories 54 Fat 0 g Carbohydrate 10 g Protein 2 g Sodium 1 mg Cholesterol 0 mg

Turkey Loaf Sandwiches

1 pound ground turkey
  breast
1 egg, slightly beaten
1 (6-ounce) can tomato
  paste
½ cup oatmeal
1 medium onion, chopped
1 teaspoon pepper
8 slices light wheat bread

Preheat oven to 325°. Combine all ingredients; shape into a small loaf pan or baking pan coated with nonstick spray. Bake for about 40 minutes. Slice into 4 servings when cool; serve on bread.

Yield: 4 sandwiches

Nutrients per sandwich:

Calories 350 Fat 3 g Carbohydrate 46 g Protein 33 g Sodium 282 mg Cholesterol 192 mg

Tropical Citrus Mix

1 medium banana, sliced
1 cup pineapple chunks
1 cup cherries, halved
1 medium grapefruit,
 peeled and sliced

Combine all ingredients, and mix well. Chill well before serving.

Yield: 8 (½-cup) servings

Nutrients per serving:

Calories 50 Fat 0 g Carbohydrate 12 g Protein 0 g Sodium 1 mg Cholesterol 0 mg

High-Energy Sparkler

2 cups sparkling grape juice
2 cups pineapple juice
2 cups seltzer water

Combine all ingredients. Serve over ice.

Yield: 6 (1-cup) servings

Nutrients per cup:

Calories 50 Fat 0 g Carbohydrate 13 g Protein 0 g Sodium 0 mg Cholesterol 0 mg

Exercise goes right along with light eating, but take it easy in the hot daytime sun with less strenuous activities.

End of School

Short Regrets

There was nothing to do but turn in books, scissors, and markers; clean out our desks; and collect the papers and doily-decorated poems from the walls. It was the last day of fifth grade, but the feeling wasn't the same as the end of other school years. They were shutting down the school. No one could deal with that.

The normal thing to do on the last day of school was to run out of our classrooms, through the halls, and out of the building...screaming for our freedom. Usually it was straight onto our bikes and down to the beach, never bothering to glance back. But that day was different; that day we lingered.

We took pictures of each other on the playground—at the place where we chased Moey Drane to kiss him in kindergarten, by the tether ball pole where Chris Peterson's tongue got stuck one winter day, and in the open area where we dug igloos in the snow with paths connecting them to one another, until someone yelled "queen of the mountain," and we piled on and collapsed the snow structures. We crowded together for the photos, our hair in ribbons, our faces painted with pink blush and blue eye shadow, our hips jutted out with attitude. We dressed up punk for the last day as a joke; however, no one really knew what punk was so it ended up being a lot of attitude. After all, they were closing *our* school.

Finally, someone reminded us that it was the first afternoon of summer, so we shoved the old erasers and notes to each other into our bags, hopped onto our bikes, and headed to Megann's for tuna sandwiches. Her mom made the best ones—with celery and pickle juice. After that, we raced down the oak-lined street to the beach, where we dropped our bikes and ran down the bluff hill so fast our feet had trouble keeping up. It had been muggy in school for weeks, but by the beach, it was windy and chilly. The beach sign stated "Lake Michigan water 47 degrees today." Despite the warnings, we plunged in...and quickly ran back out. As we sat on the beach shivering, the old school became a thing of the past as we thought about the whole summer ahead of us.

Marny Requa
Editor, **Might** *magazine*
San Francisco, CA

WRITE DOWN (OR HAVE YOUR CHILD WRITE DOWN) the 10 things that would constitute a successful summer. Accomplish (or promise your child you'll accomplish) at least 3 of the things. Keep the list in a prominent place so you can refer to it frequently. Make sure 1 of the things is something to improve yourself or improve your surroundings.

Invite your friends or your child's friends for a SPECIAL END-OF-SCHOOL PICNIC. Feed them; then head to the beach, movies, park, amusement park, or miniature golf. Let them feel like a fun summer is about to begin. They've worked hard all year—they deserve it.

If you've just finished a year at college, TREAT YOURSELF TO A WEEK-END AWAY before beginning your summer job or more studies. Lounging at the beach or camping and hiking with friends in the mountains will rejuvenate your spirits.

SUMMER SAMPLER

Creamy Vegetables on Crackers
Crunchy Raisin Salad

🍓 🍓 🍓

Summertime Egg Salad
Peppery Potato Salad

🍓 🍓 🍓

Berry Frozen Yogurt
Creamy Orange Cooler

🍓 🍓 🍓

Creamy Vegetables on Crackers

1 tablespoon chopped
   chives
1 tablespoon minced red
   bell pepper
1 tablespoon minced yellow
   bell pepper
1 (8-ounce) package light
   soft cream cheese

Mix chives and peppers with cream cheese. Serve on vegetable crackers.

Yield: about 1 cup

Nutrients per (1 tablespoon) serving:

Calories 30 Fat 2 g Carbohydrate 0 g Protein 1 g Sodium 66 mg Cholesterol 0 mg

Crunchy Raisin Salad

4 medium carrots, cut into
   thin strips
¾ cup raisins
1 large apple, chopped
1 cup fat-free honey Dijon
   mustard

Mix carrots with fruit. Add dressing before serving.

Yield: 4 servings

Nutrients per serving:

Calories 247 Fat 0 g Carbohydrate 58 g Protein 1 g Sodium 555 mg Cholesterol 0 mg

Summertime Egg Salad

6 eggs, hard cooked, peeled, and chopped
¼ cup nonfat mayonnaise
¼ cup prepared mustard
¼ cup chopped celery
2 tablespoons minced onion
2 tablespoons minced green bell pepper

Combine all ingredients. Chill before serving.

Yield: 4 servings

Nutrients per serving:

Calories 144 Fat 8 g Carbohydrate 4 g Protein 9 g Sodium 479 mg Cholesterol 322 mg

Peppery Potato Salad

3 cups cooked diced potatoes
½ cup diced green bell pepper
½ cup diced red bell pepper
¼ cup green onion slices
1 cup reduced-calorie mayonnaise

Combine vegetables. Stir in mayonnaise, and mix well.

Yield: 4 servings

Nutrients per serving:

Calories 200 Fat 13 g Carbohydrate 17 g Protein 1 g Sodium 300 mg Cholesterol 0 mg

Berry Frozen Yogurt

1 cup chopped strawberries
1 cup raspberries
1 cup blueberries
1 quart nonfat vanilla frozen yogurt, partially thawed

Combine fruits in a freezer-safe container; mix in yogurt. Return to freezer until firm.

Yield: 14 servings

Nutrients per serving:

Calories 77 Fat 0 g Carbohydrate 18 g Protein 1 g Sodium 26 mg Cholesterol 0 mg

Creamy Orange Cooler

1 (6-ounce) can orange juice concentrate
1 cup 2% milk
1 cup water
1 small orange, chopped
½ teaspoon vanilla flavor
10 ice cubes

Place all ingredients in a blender. Cover and blend until smooth.

Yield: 6 servings

Nutrients per serving:

Calories 95 Fat 1 g Carbohydrate 20 g Protein 3 g Sodium 21 mg Cholesterol 1 mg

While most adults need to be conscious of how much they eat, children are still growing and can enjoy most foods as long as meals are balanced and indulgent "goodies" are offered in moderation.

Picnic in a City Park

L'Été à Paris

Summertime in Paris. For a girl of 19, it means culture, boys, wonderment, romance. And for my best friend and me, in particular, it meant to quit existing and begin living. Our initiation into this transformation occurred on our first day in Paris. We had arrived a few days early into the city—we had exactly 72 hours to experience Paris on our own before meeting our respective host families and beginning our summer classes. We decided to christen these three days of uninhibited freedom with a picnic. "Yes," we thought, "A picnic in the Jardin des Tuileries. How Parisienne."

So we set out from our 6th arrondissement hotel toward Paris' Tuilerie Gardens, which run in back of the Louvre along the Seine River. We picked up some bread and cheese, and then stopped by a fruit stand for a pear and an apricot. (I paid $9 for that pear. It was a good pear, but its high price came not from its succulent flavor, but from our naïveté. We had unknowingly stopped at Europe's most well-known, exclusive fruit market. And because we didn't clearly understand the franc/dollar exchange rate yet, I did not realize my exorbitant purchase until 3 hours later.)

So we took our bread and our cheese and our fruit, and we found a bench. Our bench was surrounded by trees that formed a square, and we all—us and the trees—faced inward toward a nude in stone. We sat on that bench for hours, sometimes laughing, sometimes talking, sometimes just sitting. I don't remember what I wrote in my journal that day; Jennifer doesn't remember what she drew in her sketch book. But we do remember Marie, the fish monger, who asked Jennifer to marry him within the first four minutes of meeting. We remember the old French man who, with his decrepit bicycle, fresh baguette, and navy-blue beret, chose us as models for his next painting. We remember the young mothers with their rosy-cheeked little boys, navigating their toy boats in the fountain. We remember the state of unbelief that we were actually in Paris. And we remember most the excitement, the fear of the summer to come.

Martha Hopkins
Memphis, TN

WHAT BETTER WAY TO DISCOVER A NEW CITY (and it doesn't have to be very far away) and its people and their habits than to picnic in one of its central parks. Just be sure to find out from your hotel staff or the local authorities where a good safe location may be. Most towns and cities have green areas downtown where you can enjoy the experience.

SOME SUGGESTIONS FOR PICNICS IN CITIES you may be visiting include the Boston Commons; The Mall in Washington, D.C., which is bordered by the museums of the Smithsonian Institute; the squares of Savannah, where you can observe the architecture of this lovely Georgian city.

LUNCH AND LEARN

Tangy Cucumber Spears
Snow Pea Salad

❦ ❦ ❦

Garden Macaroni Salad
Marinated Turkey Breast Sandwich

❦ ❦ ❦

Grapefruit Surprise
Sunset Punch

❦ ❦ ❦

Tangy Cucumber Spears

4 medium cucumbers
2 cups nonfat red wine and vinegar dressing
1 cup finely chopped red bell pepper
1 teaspoon black pepper

Cut cucumbers in half, then cut each half into four spears. Combine dressing, bell pepper, and black pepper. Pour dressing mixture over cucumber spears, and marinate several hours before serving:

Yield: 8 servings

Nutrients per serving:

Calories 62 g Fat 0 g Carbohydrate 12 g Protein 1 g Sodium 800 mg Cholesterol 0 mg

Snow Pea Salad

2 cups snow peas
½ cup red bell pepper slices
1 tablespoon soy sauce
2 teaspoons sesame oil
1 teaspoon ground ginger
1 teaspoon garlic powder

Steam snow peas and red bell pepper until tender. Combine soy sauce, sesame oil, and spices. Sprinkle over peas and pepper slices.

Yield: 4 servings

Nutrients per serving:

Calories 63 g Fat 2 g Carbohydrate 8 g Protein 4 g Sodium 260 mg Cholesterol 0 mg

Garden Macaroni Salad

2 cups cooked, drained macaroni
2 cups zucchini slices
2 cups mushroom halves
½ cup red onion rings
1 (8-ounce) bottle nonfat red wine and vinegar dressing

Combine first 4 ingredients; toss with dressing.

Yield: 4 servings

Nutrients per serving:

Calories 132 Fat 0 g Carbohydrate 25 g Protein 6 g Sodium 18 mg Cholesterol 0 mg

Marinated Turkey Breast Sandwich

½ cup balsamic vinegar
1 tablespoon lemon juice
1 tablespoon parsley
1 teaspoon black pepper
1 pound turkey breast slices
4 kaiser rolls
Lettuce and tomato (optional)

Combine vinegar, lemon juice, parsley and pepper. Pour over turkey in shallow dish, and marinate in refrigerator 1 hour or longer. Remove turkey from marinade, and grill until tender. Serve grilled turkey breast slices in rolls; garnish with lettuce and tomato, if desired.

Yield: 4 sandwiches

Nutrients per sandwich:

Calories 288 g Fat 5 g Carbohydrate 30 g Protein 30 g Sodium 367 mg Cholesterol 59 mg

Grapefruit Surprise

8 medium strawberries,
  halved
1 cup red grapes, halved
3 grapefruit, halved

Combine strawberries and grapes. Top each grapefruit half with one-sixth of mixture.

Yield: 6 servings

Nutrients per serving:

Calories 75 g Fat 0 g Carbohydrate 19 g Protein 1 g Sodium 0 mg Cholesterol 0 mg

Sunset Punch

1 quart orange juice
½ quart grape juice
½ quart apple juice
1 quart diet 7 up
2 cups seltzer water

Mix juices, soda, and seltzer together in a large container. Serve over ice.

Yield: approximately 18 (6-ounce) servings

Nutrients per serving:

Calories 50 g Fat 0 g Carbohydrate 12 mg Protein 0 g Sodium 0 mg Cholesterol 0 mg

Light foods energize you without weighing you down from fun in the sun.

Horseback Riding

Horseback Writing

I remember the first time I touched a horse. I was wearing white sandals with no socks. I stood waist high to my father in a field that shimmered with sun and bees. Eyes down, I tiptoed oh so carefully through the clover, begging not to be stung. But my fear vanished when I saw the horses—three or four of them, one a baby. Talking softly, Daddy pressed my hand into its velvety back. I looked into the largest eyes I'd ever seen. Something shifted in me. I had touched wildness. The door to my imagination blew open. Before scrawling a single word, I had become a writer.

I soon discovered "Roy Rogers" and "Fury" on TV. I sat front-row to westerns at the local theater. I had an imaginary palomino in my yard. Then came elation—a chance to climb on a *real* horse, actually a shaggy Shetland pony. I loved the creak of the leather saddle, the challenge of the stirrups, the power of holding both reins in *one* hand. My faithful companion and I thundered through imaginary canyons chasing the "bad guys." I clung to the vision all day, my clothes rich with the scent of sweaty horses and hay.

Even now, it's that sweet musty fragrance that conjures up memorable rides: cantering through towering Wisconsin woods, riding tandem with my children in Hawaii, spying deer on a misty trek through Tennessee's Cade's Cove.

Several autumns ago, I sojourned in the North Georgia mountains, letting the coiling road lead me wherever. I saw a weathered sign: Horseback Riding. I roared past the sagging barn, with its horsey aroma. After 2 miles, I turned around.

The lanky guide didn't look a thing like my father. But for an hour, as we crunched through the scarlet-and-gold woodland, he talked about his daughters. One wrote poetry. He wasn't sure how to encourage her. The broad, brown neck of my horse grew warm and wet. The saddle creaked. The reins loosened in my hand. Insects buzzed. I felt a kinship with this yearning teenager I'd never meet. I thanked him for the ride, handing him a book for her on writing called *Wild Mind*. He took it awkwardly, not quite understanding. I felt sure his daughter would.

I drove off, smelling of sweaty leather and hay, and realizing that riding horses and writing were two of the wildest things I'd ever do.

Isabelle V. Hanson
Birmingham, AL

FOR $10 YOU CAN PURCHASE the paperback version of *Wild Mind: Living the Writer's Life* by Natalie Goldberg (Bantam Press). Ask for it at your local bookstore.

KENTUCKY HORSE PARK IN LEXINGTON provides a fun day for horse enthusiasts. There are live shows, a museum, barn tours, 1-hour guided trail rides, and much more. For details, write to Kentucky Horse Park, 4089 Iron Works Pike, Lexington, KY 40511.

TAKE A HORSEBACK RIDING TRIP. Many state and national parks offer horseback riding as part of their programs. Or for a longer trip, try the Flying L Guest Ranch, 542 acres located in Bandera in the beautiful Hill Country of Texas, offers horseback riding to your heart's content, in addition to golf, tennis, swimming, children's activities, and much more. Call 1-800-292-5134 for details.

In North Carolina, CATALOOCHEE RANCH SCHEDULES ONLY MEALS AND HORSEBACK RIDING. However, you can also hike, swim, play tennis, and explore many other options. All this is in Maggie Valley, in the southwest area of the state. For more information, call 1-800-868-1401.

IF YOU'RE INTO RIDING OF A DIFFERENT NATURE and are planning a trip to the Grand Canyon, consider mule rides down into the canyon. You can experience the day trip or even the overnight package where you stay in cabins at the Phantom Ranch. Be adventuresome; call (601) 638-2401.

R E I N   I N   S U P P E R

Onion Relish
Kaleidoscope Salad

🐎 🐎 🐎

Breezy Crabmeat Salad
Vegetable-Stuffed Pitas

🐎 🐎 🐎

Apple Raisin Cookies
Raspberry Spiked Tea

🐎 🐎 🐎

Onion Relish

½ cup chopped red onion
½ cup chopped white onion
½ teaspoon black pepper
1 teaspoon prepared
   mustard
1 tablespoon cider vinegar

Combine all ingredients. Mix well. Use as a spread on sandwiches, hot dogs, or hamburgers.

Yield: about 1½ cups

Nutrients per tablespoon:

Calories 4 Fat 0 g Carbohydrate 1 g Protein 0 g Sodium 4 mg Cholesterol 0 mg

Kaleidoscope Salad

12 ounces cooked top round
   steak, cut into strips
1 cup nonfat red wine
   vinegar dressing
1 cup shredded purple
   cabbage
½ cup red onion, thinly
   sliced
1 cup zucchini squash strips
1 teaspoon horseradish

In large bowl, marinate beef strips in dressing several hours or overnight. Add remaining ingredients. Chill before serving.

Yield: 4 servings

Nutrients per serving:

Calories 187 Fat 4 g Carbohydrate 5 g Protein 26 mg Sodium 816 mg Cholesterol 60 mg

Using mashed or pureed fruits are wonderful ways to replace fat while adding flavor, color, and variety to baked goods, such as cookies, cakes, and muffins.

Breezy Crabmeat Salad

16 ounces imitation
   crabmeat chunks
½ cup nonfat tartar sauce
¼ cup chopped onion
1 tablespoon salt-free lemon
   pepper seasoning
½ cup zucchini slices
½ cup cut green beans

*Combine all ingredients. Chill
before serving.*

Yield: 4 servings

Nutrients per serving:

Calories 157 Fat 1 g Carbohydrate 26 g Protein 13 g Sodium 1165 mg Cholesterol 21 mg

Vegetable-Stuffed Pitas

4 pita bread halves
1 cup carrot slices
2 tomatoes, sliced
1 Spanish onion, sliced
1 cup radish slices
1 cup zucchini, sliced
¼ cup nonfat red wine
   vinegar dressing
4 teaspoons black pepper

*Fill each pita bread half with ¼
cup carrot slices, 3 tomato slices,
¼ cup onion slices, ¼ cup radish
slices, ¼ cup zucchini slices.
Drizzle with 1 tablespoon dressing, and sprinkle 1 teaspoon
pepper on top. (Prior to filling
pitas, spread each with Onion
Relish, if desired.)*

Yield: 4 stuffed pita pockets

Nutrients per pita pocket:

Calories 150 Fat 1 g Carbohydrate 30 g Protein 4 g Sodium 390 mg Cholesterol 0 mg

Apple Raisin Cookies

¾ cup applesauce
½ cup sugar
1 egg
1½ cups flour
½ cup whole wheat flour
1 teaspoon baking powder
1 teaspoon vanilla extract
¾ cup raisins

Preheat oven to 350°. In a large bowl, mix applesauce and sugar. Add egg, and beat well. Stir in flours, baking powder, vanilla, and raisins; mix until well combined. Drop dough by generous teaspoonfuls onto greased cookie sheet. Bake about 10 minutes or until lightly browned. Let stand for a few minutes before removing from baking sheet; cookies will become slightly firmer upon cooling. Store in an airtight container.

Note: Fat-free cookies require slightly less cooking time than typical for drop cookie dough. Larger cookie dough portions prevent dryness upon cooling.

Yield: about 2 dozen cookies

Nutrients per cookie:

Calories 71 Fat 0 g Carbohydrate 16 g Protein 2 g Sodium 17 g Cholesterol 9 mg

Raspberry Spiked Tea

1 (4-serving) package raspberry gelatin
2 quarts unsweetened iced tea

Lightly coat ice cube trays with nonstick spray. Prepare gelatin mix per package; pour into ice cube trays. Cover and freeze. Add frozen cubes to "take-along" containers of ice tea.

Nutrients per 1 cup:

Calories 40 Fat 0 g Carbohydrate 10 g Protein 1 g Sodium 25 mg Cholesterol 0 mg

Sunday Drives

Sunday Memories

Sunday afternoon drives were a tradition in my family. Almost every weekend my parents packed all six kids into the blue Chevrolet and headed out for an excursion. Often we cruised down Riverside Drive along the River Bluffs. Daddy loved to show us the Indian Mounds where he had played as a boy; our eyes never left the ground searching for arrowheads like he had found. No trip was complete without Daddy driving toward the edge of the bluff pretending that the Chevy's brakes had failed. As we screamed and clung to the back seat, Mama admonished Daddy and tried not to laugh.

Another favorite drive was to Mama's Aunt Sperinda and Uncle Johnny's house in the country. For me, the highlight of the trip was their mule, Sam. I was fascinated by those extra-long ears and the way he stood so solemnly in the pasture, as inscrutable as the Sphinx. I wondered what old Sam could possibly be thinking as I patiently fed him hay through the fence; then someone always made me come into the house to eat my own dinner.

Although a mule is surely a compelling attraction for any child, it seems hard to believe that I considered passing up my aunt's homemade gnocchi (Italian potato dumplings), smothered in butter and sprinkled generously with freshly grated Parmesan cheese. Not to mention dessert, which was usually bowties, crusty, Italian pastries dusted with powdered sugar and much-loved by the children in our family.

Uncle Johnny's contribution to the meal was delicious dry, red, Italian wine made in his basement. Aunt Sperinda always insisted that Mama let us kids have some wine, too. Not just a sip, mind you, but our own glass "like the children back in Italy." As Aunt Sperinda poured the wine, Mama also poured water into the small glasses. Personally, I considered these wine-tastings to be surpassed only by the feeding of hay to Sam.

Aunt Sperinda had a way of convincing Mama when it came to most things. Prior to one of our visits, my great aunt's dog had puppies. Despite Mama and Daddy's protests, when we piled back into the car that afternoon, there were three new passengers. Full of gnocchi and bowties, my two older sisters and I each happily held our very own puppy during the drive home.

Lisa Brinda
Memphis, TN

GO ESTATE SALE SHOPPING. Necessary ingredients: car, map, Sunday want-ads (and the funny papers, in case you get bored), cash, comfortable shoes. Hint: On the second day of a sale (i.e., Sunday) you have great bargaining power.

 FIND SOME ENLIGHTENING STREETS TO EXPLORE: **Memphis**— Belvedere, with its big old houses; **Los Angeles**—Mulholland Drive, to search for the stars; **Lancaster** (PA)—two-lane country roads off Route 23, for a true glance at Amish life; **Dallas**—McKinney, for some of the best restaurants and shops in the city (drive along it first; then pick your spot and take a stroll).

 TAKE ALONG BABY WIPES (for everyone's hands), tapes for the car to help set the mood (sing-along tapes if the kids are with you), a blanket (to spread out the picnic), and a camera (for any exciting sights along the way).

A F T E R - T H E - D R I V E   D E L I G H T S

Deviled Eggs
Clear-Day Potato Salad

❧ ❧ ❧

Picnic Chicken
Pea and Rice Salad

❧ ❧ ❧

Fruity Sugar Cookies
Tart 'n' Tangy Raspberry Sparkler

❧ ❧ ❧

.

Deviled Eggs

6 eggs, hardcooked
½ cup nonfat mayonnaise
¼ cup prepared mustard
2 tablespoon minced onion
1 tablespoon chopped
   parsley
1 teaspoon black pepper
Paprika

Cut eggs lengthwise. Remove yolks from whites. Mash yolks, and combine with mayonnaise, mustard, onion, parsley, and pepper. Refill each cooked egg white half with a spoonful of creamed yolk mixture. Sprinkle with paprika before serving.

Yield: 12 deviled eggs

Nutrients per 2:

Calories 105 Fat 5 g Carbohydrate 6 g Protein 6 g Sodium 441 mg Cholesterol 215 mg

Clear-Day Potato Salad

4 medium potatoes, cooked
   and cubed
1 cup balsamic vinegar
¼ cup chopped parsley
1 cup green onion
1 teaspoon black pepper
1 tablespoon prepared
   mustard
1 teaspoon minced garlic

Combine all ingredients. Chill before serving.

Yield: 6 servings

Nutrients per serving:

Calories 86 Fat 0 g Carbohydrate 19 g Protein 2 g Sodium 133 mg Cholesterol 0 mg

Eating less fat can be quite tasty once you learn some simple tips of seasoning.

Picnic Chicken

1½ cups breadcrumbs
1½ teaspoons parsley
1½ teaspoons onion powder
1½ teaspoons oregano
1½ teaspoons black pepper
1½ pounds boneless, skinless
   chicken breasts
¾ cup plain nonfat yogurt
Nonstick cooking spray

Preheat oven to 350°. Combine first 5 ingredients; mix well, and set aside. Moisten chicken in yogurt. Coat with breadcrumb-seasoning mixture. Spray shallow baking pan with cooking spray. Arrange chicken breasts in pan, and bake in oven 30 minutes or until fork tender.

Yield: 6 servings

Nutrients per serving:

Calories 230 Fat 3 g Carbohydrate 20 g Protein 28 g Sodium 267 mg Cholesterol 73 mg

Pea and Rice Salad

1 cup cooked brown rice
1 cup cooked peas
1 cup mushrooms
½ cup green onions, thinly
   sliced
Fat-free dressing

Toss all ingredients together. Serve cold with choice of dressing.

Yield: 6 servings

Nutrients per serving:

Calories 59 Fat 0 g Carbohydrate 11g Protein 2 g Sodium 72 g Cholesterol 0 mg

If you want to add some wine like Aunt Sperinda and Uncle Johnny always do, try Brolio Chianti from the Tuscany region of Italy—it's a good mid-price-range wine that would be perfect for the occasion.

Fruity Sugar Cookies

2 cups flour
1½ teaspoons baking soda
¼ cup applesauce
¼ cup margarine, softened
¾ cup sugar
1 teaspoon vanilla extract
1 egg yolk

Preheat oven to 350°. In small bowl, combine flour and baking soda; set aside. In large bowl, beat applesauce, margarine, sugar, and vanilla; add egg yolk. Stir in flour mixture. Chill until firm. Shape dough into 1-inch balls; place 2 inches apart on lightly greased baking sheet. Flatten. Bake for 8 minutes or until lightly browned.

Yield: about 2½ dozen

Nutrients per cookie:

Calories 55 Fat 2 g Carbohydrate 9 g Protein 1 g Sodium 57 mg Cholesterol 7 mg

Tart 'n' Tangy Raspberry Sparkler

1 (10-ounce) package frozen raspberries, thawed
1 (6-ounce) package frozen orange juice concentrate, thawed
1 (1-liter) bottle diet lemon-lime soda
1 (1-liter) bottle seltzer water

Combine ingredients in blender; blend until smooth.

Yield: 8 servings

Nutrients per serving:

Calories 50 Fat 0 g Carbohydrate 12 g Protein 0 g Sodium 0 mg Cholesterol 0 g

Bird Watching

Texas Bird Watching

There is no finer experience than to go bird watching on the Texas Coast in late April. Choose a day after a powerful cold front has come through—the wilder the better. All that thunder and lightning and energy goes across the Texas coast into the Gulf of Mexico where it meets the spring migration of songbirds coming north from Central and South America.

The migration of these birds is a natural wonder. They have spent the winter in the tropical rainforest and are now returning for the summer. Mating is the first order of business and the songbirds' breeding colors are in full display.

A day or two after a cold front has passed is the best time because these travellers become exhausted from fighting the turbulence and literally "fall out" along the coast. There are tales of these birds being so drained that they land on the beach by the thousands, but such occasions are truly rare. More commonly, these birds seek the first wooded areas near the shoreline, and there are several key "woodlots" on the Texas coast where these gorgeous migrants gather.

A magical experience awaits those lucky birders entering these woodlots where living ornaments adorn the trees. Excitement is in the air as groups of birders shout each new species discovered. Here's a black-throated blue; there's a redstart. The mulberries are like honey to the scarlet-coated tanagers and red-breasted grosbeaks, while yellow-and black-flecked warblers chase insects down the limbs. Northern and orchard orioles turn a live oak orange and black while indigo buntings reflect a startling blue as they browse for seeds. And the sly old cat bird slips through the brambles, wisely watching the watchers.

At the end of the day, a comforting peace settles over the group. The spiritual connection between humans and other living species is clear after birding the Texas coast in the spring.

Jim Blackburn
Houston, TX

There are several WELL-KNOWN COASTAL WOODLOTS around Galveston Bay where the spring migrations can be seen. The Houston Audubon Society operates a sanctuary in High Island, Texas, and the Texas Parks and Wildlife Commission operates a sanctuary in Smith Point, Texas. Many of the local parks on Galveston Island and farther down the coast also provide habitat for these migrants. Migrants can be seen most anytime from mid-April to mid-May, it's just better after a storm.

TO BIRD WATCH, you need binoculars and a camera with a telephoto lens (if you wish to capture it on film). An identification guide is a help if you see some birds that you are unfamiliar with. Bird watching is a quiet activity, so take along lots of patience and you will be rewarded with the glories of nature.

Chirp for Lunch

Garden Vegetable Dipper
Broccoli Rice Salad
Marinated Cauliflower

🐦 🐦 🐦

Light 'n' Cheesy Lunch

🐦 🐦 🐦

Tropical Summer Fruit Salad
Tart Iced Tea

🐦 🐦 🐦

Garden Vegetable Dipper

8 ounces nonfat yogurt
½ cup nonfat mayonnaise
dressing
1 tablespoon minced onion
½ teaspoon crushed oregano
¼ teaspoon garlic pepper
¼ teaspoon black pepper

Combine all ingredients; mix well. Serve with raw vegetables as dippers.

Yield: about 1½ cups

Nutrients per tablespoon:

Calories 24 Fat 0 g Carbohydrate 5 g Protein 0 g Sodium 125 mg Cholesterol 0 mg

Broccoli Rice Salad

1 cup blanched chopped
broccoli
1 cup cooked rice
¼ cup minced red bell
pepper
Nonfat Italian dressing

Combine broccoli, rice, and bell pepper. Serve with nonfat dressing.

Yield: about 4 (½-cup) servings

Nutrients per serving:

Calories 52 Fat 0 g Carbohydrate 22 g Protein 4 g Sodium 147 mg Cholesterol 0 mg

Smaller meals with light snacks offers one approach to lighthearted eating.

Marinated Cauliflower

2 cups cauliflower pieces
1 cup red wine vinegar
1 tablespoon chopped
   parsley

Combine all ingredients; marinate several hours or overnight.

Yield: about 4 (½-cup) servings

Nutrients per serving:

Calories 18 Fat 0 g Carbohydrate 3 g Protein 2 g Sodium 45 mg Cholesterol 0 mg

Light 'n' Cheesy Lunch

1 teaspoon olive oil
¼ cup cider vinegar
⅛ teaspoon garlic powder
¼ teaspoon onion powder
8 ounces nonfat mozzarella
   cheese slices
8 tomato slices

Mix olive oil, vinegar, and seasoning together. On serving platter, partially stack cheese and tomato slices, alternating the two. Drizzle with oil and vinegar mixture.

Yield: 4 servings

Nutrients per serving:

Calories 108 Fat 2 g Carbohydrate 5 g Protein 17 g Sodium 485 mg Cholesterol 10 mg

Tropical Summer Fruit Salad

1 cup pineapple chunks
1 cup pink grapefruit
  sections
1 cup green grape halves

Combine all ingredients; chill before serving.

Yield: 6 (½-cup) servings

Nutrients per serving:

Calories 42 Fat 0 g Carbohydrate 10 g Protein 0 g Sodium 2 mg Cholesterol 0 mg

Tart Iced Tea

3 quarts water
4 tea bags
¾ cup lime juice
Sugar to taste

Boil water; pour over tea bags in heat-resistant pitcher. Steep for 5 minutes. Remove tea bags; add lime juice. Chill and serve over ice. Sweeten with sugar.

Yield: 12¾ cups

Nutrients per cup:

Calories 4 Fat 0 g Carbohydrate 1 g Protein 0 g Sodium 0 mg Cholesterol 0 mg

Scuba Diving

Old Wise Man of the Sea

A plume of diesel faded into the landscape as the dive boat headed out the inlet into open water, the horizon widening with every gentle roll from port to starboard. It was only then that I noticed that we were the only divers who had two tanks.

We had driven nearly an hour up the South Florida coast to dive this reef and assumed that we would get two dives for our money. Chagrined, we found out that the Palm Beach diving club was so close to the inlet that it opted for multiple single tank trips rather than only a couple of two-tank outings. My dive buddy, Steve, became somewhat edgy on that news.

The boat quickly arrived at the dive site, and the dive master briefed us. In no time, everyone was geared and jumping in the warm, summer water. Joking with me earlier, Steve quipped that he would never have a problem locating me underwater because of my neon green wet suit and flippers. That day, nine other divers were wearing neon green.

We descended to about 70 feet in the clear blue water and swam to the edge of a tropical fish paradise. The brilliant teal of the parrot fish, the surreal size of round filters, the patience of a giant, emerald moray eel waiting for a victim to break through his blindness—all made us feel as if we were interlopers, gawking tourists who could never assimilate into his harmonious world.

Out of the corner of my eye, I saw a large shadow on a ledge below us. I motioned to the others. Dropping to 90 feet, we circled around the creature, apparently asleep. It was a loggerhead sea turtle, a close relative to the endangered leatherback turtle. As large as an office desk and weighing 400 to 500 pounds, the turtle slowly opened one eye and stared at us.

I suddenly felt that terrible sense of awkwardness and anxiety that I felt when I was a child, at times of spilling grape juice on the neighbor's ivory carpet or walking into a room where someone was dressing.

We had jarred the old, wise man of the sea from his rest. Yet we hovered, awestruck, and could do nothing but stare in return.

Barry McCann
Pompano Beach, FL

TO PARTICIPATE IN SCUBA DIVING, you must have appropriate certification, which usually includes four check-out dives. For information on how to obtain certification, call a dive shop in a city near you.

 FOR A UNIQUE EXPERIENCE FROM DECEMBER THROUGH MARCH, you can swim (snorkel or scuba dive) with the manatees in Crystal River, Florida. For details, write Nature Coast Chamber of Commerce, 28 Northwest Highway 19, Crystal River, FL 34428.

 FOR SOME OF THE BEST PLACES TO SCUBA DIVE because of clear water, abundant fish life, and variety of fish life, call your travel agent and plan a trip to Belize, Little Cayman, or Cozumel.

D I V E   I N T O   D I N N E R

Cheesy Popcorn
Blazing Coleslaw

🐸 🐸 🐸

Colorful Macaroni Salad
High Seas Salad

🐸 🐸 🐸

Spiced Peaches
High Seas Sparkler

🐸 🐸 🐸

Cheesy Popcorn

8 cups freshly popped corn
¼ cup (52%) vegetable oil
   spread, melted
¼ cup grated Parmesan
   cheese

Toss popcorn with spread and cheese. Serve warm.

Yield: 8 cups

Nutrients per cup:

Calories 73 Fat 5 g Carbohydrate 5 g Protein 3 g Sodium 75 mg Cholesterol 0 mg

Blazing Coleslaw

1 quart shredded red
   cabbage
½ cup chopped red bell
   pepper
¼ cup chopped red onion
½ cup light mayonnaise

Combine first 3 ingredients; mix lightly. Chill. Add mayonnaise before serving.

Yield: 6 servings

Nutrients per ½ cup:

Calories 71 Fat 4 g Carbohydrate 7 g Protein 1 g Sodium 118 mg Cholesterol 0 mg

Summertime often means a fresh harvest of seafood, many of which are naturally lower in fat.

Colorful Macaroni Salad

2 cups cooked elbow
  macaroni
2 medium tomatoes
1 cup nonfat plain yogurt
½ cup chopped green
  pepper
¼ cup chopped onion
½ teaspoon garlic powder

*Combine all ingredients; mix
well. Chill before serving.*

Yield: 6 servings

Nutrients per serving:

Calories 116 Fat 0 g Carbohydrate 23 g Protein 4 g Sodium 27 mg Cholesterol 0 mg

High Seas Salad

8 ounces imitation
  crabmeat flakes
8 ounces imitation lobster
  chunks
½ cup nonfat mayonnaise
1½ teaspoons salt-free lemon
  pepper seasoning
½ cup chopped celery
½ cup chopped green bell
  pepper

*Combine all ingredients; mix
well. Chill before serving.*

Yield: 4 servings

Nutrients per serving:

Calories 140 Fat 1 g Carbohydrate 16 g Protein 17 g Sodium 568 mg Cholesterol 31 mg

Spiced Peaches

2 tablespoons sugar
½ teaspoon cinnamon
4 medium peaches, cubed
1 cup cherries, halved

Toss sugar with cinnamon. Combine peaches with sugar mixture; stir in cherries.

Yield: about 6 (½-cup) servings

Nutrients per serving:

Calories 53 Fat 0 g Carbohydrate 14 g Protein 0 g Sodium 0 mg Cholesterol 0 mg

High Seas Sparkler

2 cups sparkling grape juice
2 cups orange juice
2 cups seltzer water

Combine all ingredients. Serve over ice.

Yield: 6 cups

Nutrients per cup:

Calories 40 Fat 0 g Carbohydrate 10 g Protein 0 g Sodium 0 mg Cholesterol 0 mg

Camping

Away From It All

The clanging six o'clock dinnerbell echoed off the mountains, sending urban cowboys and cowgirls from their cabins to the lodge dining room. Meals were served family style, and we usually sat with different people each time, all happy to be more than 8,000 feet above sea level in the Colorado Rockies, away from it all.

The owner of Drowsy Water Ranch stood and announced an overnight mountaintop campout the following evening for those who were interested. Herb, a jovial veteran ranch guest from Minnesota who was sitting across from us, said to everyone at our table, "You've got to do the overnight. Sleeping out under the stars, so close to the heavens, is an experience you'll never forget."

"Can we Mom? Please?" my 6- and 8-year-old sons pleaded in unison.

Late the following afternoon, we were on our horses climbing the mountain, along with Herb, of course, and 14 others. Halfway into our trek, clouds rolled over, obscuring the mid-August sun. "Grab the slickers tied behind your saddles," called the lead wrangler. Within minutes, hail pelted down. I thought surely we would head back to shelter at the ranch when the hail turned to rain, but our surefooted, hardy trail horses plodded on along the muddy, rocky terrain they knew so well. *Clunk. Clunk. Clunk.* The rain ended when we finally reached our mountaintop campsite. Herb jumped off his horse and kissed the ground, while the rest of us laughed, sharing in his relief.

We were thirsty, so the wrangler showed us a bubbling mountain spring. I'll never forget the fresh after-the-rain scent of overhanging evergreens as I drank the best water I've ever tasted.

There on top of that mountain in Colorado, our international camping group, who had met only days before, melted away the chilly twilight dampness. While the children scampered about gathering firewood, the adults worked together preparing a stick-to-your-ribs campfire dinner over the crackling logs. After many tall tales, jokes, and plenty of laughter, we snuggled into our sleeping bags, warm from memories of the evening.

Lying there without my contact lenses, I couldn't tell if we were near the heavens. But from the glow of the dwindling campfire, I could see my boys sleeping contentedly, and I felt we were pretty close.

Cathey Frei
Vienna, Virginia

DROWSY WATER RANCH is near Granby, Colorado, about 90 miles west of Denver. It's a Western vacation second to none. For more information, write to P.O. Box 147, Granby, CO 80446; or call 1-800-845-2292.

 GO CAMPING AMERICA COMMITTEE, out of Reston, Virginia, offers a vacation planner—a free guide to happy camping throughout the United States. To obtain the 16-page planner, call 1-800-477-8669.

 CREATE THIS MENU FOR YOUR FAMILY OR FRIENDS either in your own backyard or in a nearby state or national park that allows camping. Then settle in for an evening or songs and stories around the campfire followed by a good night's sleep in a tent or in your sleeping bag under the stars.

C A M P   R O U N D   U P

Crunchy Trail Mix

🐾 🐾 🐾

Summer Spuds
Catch-o'-the-Day Flounder
Camping Trip Baked Beans

🐾 🐾 🐾

Carameled Popcorn Balls
Lemony Strawberry Drink

🐾 🐾 🐾

Crunchy Trail Mix

2 cups mini pretzel twists
4 cups mini shredded-wheat
squares
2 cups mini popcorn cakes
2 cups raisins

Combine all ingredients. Store in airtight containers or sealed bags.

Yield: about 10 cups

Nutrients per cup:

Calories 196 Fat 0 g Carbohydrate 48 g Protein 3 g Sodium 117 mg Cholesterol 0 mg

Summer Spuds

4 large white potatoes
¼ cup chopped chives
¼ cup chopped pimiento
1 tablespoon black pepper

Wrap potatoes in foil. Cook over grill or campfire until fork tender. Open foil, and cut potatoes lengthwise. Scoop out center, and mix with remaining ingredients. Refill potatoes with mixture, close foil wrapping, and return to heat for 5 more minutes.

Yield: 4 servings

Nutrients per serving:

Calories 116 Fat 0 g Carbohydrate 25 g Protein 3 g Sodium 10 mg Cholesterol 0 g

Catch-o'-the-Day Flounder

¼ cup diet margarine
1 teaspoon black pepper
1 pound flounder, cleaned
   and boned
1 onion, sliced
1 lemon, sliced

In frying pan over low heat, melt margarine. Stir in black pepper. Add flounder and onion slices. Sauté flounder until it flakes easily with a fork. Serve with lemon slices.

Yield: 4 servings

Nutrients per serving:

Calories 99 Fat 1 g Carbohydrate 0 g Protein 21 g Sodium 89 mg Cholesterol 58 mg

Camping Trip Baked Beans

2 cups cooked red kidney
   beans
1 cup chopped onion
2 tablespoons barbecue
   sauce
2 cups tomato sauce
2 tablespoons molasses

Combine all ingredients in a 2-quart saucepan. Cover and cook over grill or campfire 30 to 35 minutes or until onion is tender and mixture is thoroughly heated. Serve hot.

Yield: 4 servings

Nutrients per serving:

Calories 93 Fat 0 g Carbohydrate 19 g Protein 4 g Sodium 626 mg Cholesterol 0 mg

With outdoor fun away from refrigerators, use coolers with plenty of ice for perishable items.

Carameled Popcorn Balls

⅓ cup light brown sugar
¼ cup water
1 tablespoon skim milk
4 cups air-popped popcorn

Dissolve brown sugar in water in a small saucepan; bring to a boil while stirring constantly. When mixture reaches a boil, stop stirring until mixture begins to thicken, about 5 minutes. Remove from heat; stir in milk. Cool slightly; then pour over popcorn. Form balls with lightly greased hands.

Yield: about 4 balls

Nutrients per serving:

Calories 103 Fat 0 g Carbohydrate 25 g Protein 0 g Sodium 8 mg Cholesterol 0 mg

Lemony Strawberry Drink

1 (4-serving) package
   strawberry gelatin
2 quarts water
¼ cup lemon juice

Lightly coat ice cube trays with nonstick spray. Prepare gelatin mix per package; pour into ice cube trays. Cover and freeze. Mix lemon juice with water. Add frozen cubes to "take-along" containers of lemon water.

Nutrients per (1 cup) serving:

Calories 40 Fat 0 g Carbohydrate 10 g Protein 1 g Sodium 25 mg Cholesterol 0 mg

Family Reunions

PASHUR

Relatives En Masse

As far back as my "memory bank" can recall, once a year our family has a reunion. Relatives travel to catch up on news, share stories and photos, and just plain relax and enjoy the fellowship. It's one of those carefree days you wish would somehow magically lengthen itself to allow a few extra hours.

During my childhood years, the car ride to our destination seemed endless, and when we'd finally arrive, I'd race to join my cousins frolicking in the day's sun. A popular spot was the huge swingset, which begged us to reach the clouds with our toes. In one corner of the park stood a gigantic sliding board. We'd carefully climb the metal stairs and then squarely place a piece of waxed paper under our seats, creating a super fast glide to the bottom. There was always a strategically positioned dust puddle waiting for us at the bottom.

The shoe scramble was also a tradition that always ended the same. My one cousin, who was rather large for his age, would leap, sprawl on the mounded shoes, and declare "king of the mountain" until he found his. We didn't mind because the yearly sight was part of the fun.

The famous peanut scramble topped off the afternoon. We'd all clutch our paper bags and scurry to catch the raining peanuts. There was always a painted peanut to indicate an extra-special prize. With all my scrambling experiences over the years, I never did capture that special nut.

Finally, we heard the words we anticipated all day—"dinner's ready." As we hurriedly entered the pavilion, an aroma of assorted goodies met us. I would eagerly take my place with my folks at one of the long tables, and pause to give thanks. Then the seemingly never-ending parade of passing food would begin—bowls filled with salads, homemade applesauce, baked beans, pickles, and fresh fruit. And then pies, cakes, brownies, and cookies would appear—all to be washed down with freshly squeezed lemonade and mint tea.

Naturally, I had to sample each delicacy—which is how I came to learn the expression, "your eyes are bigger than your stomach." When I first heard these words, I thought my parents had somehow acquired X-ray vision. Although my cousins were always finished with their meals long before me, I never minded lingering at the table to savor each bite.

Finally after hugs and long goodbyes, we would all climb into our cars for the ride home, totally exhausted but with the secure feeling that we would repeat this gathering next year. Though our family has changed, each year brings new twigs on our family tree. But the special family reunion ingredients remain constant—good food, fun, and fellowship.

Janice Wenger
Willow Street, PA

KEEP AN ANNUAL AT EACH REUNION. Have each person enter something in it that had happened to him/her during that past year (include the children's comments). Then continue the book from year to year, keeping a running record of family happenings.

 Have everyone WRITE DOWN A CARE OR WORRY that has been bothering them. Take all the papers and bury them in a deep hole—bury your troubles.

 Family reunions are GREAT TIMES TO SHARE GENEALOGY or build on a family tree. Usually someone in a family has been exploring the family history. If not, appoint someone to get started. The best place is with the elder members at the reunion. They are the significant sources for beginning such a process. After that, your local library can direct you in beginning the process. Many of them have genealogy divisions. For more information, contact National Archives and Records Service, Research Services Branch, General Services Administration, Washington, D.C. 20408.

R E U N I O N   F A R E

Layered Bean Dip
Corn Salad

🍎 🍎 🍎

Family Reunion London Broil
Sweet Pepper Salad

🍎 🍎 🍎

Chunky Fruit Mousse
Berry Sparkling Slush

🍎 🍎 🍎

Layered Bean Dip

1 cup pureed kidney beans
1 medium tomato, chopped
½ cup chopped onion
4 ounces reduced-fat
  Cheddar cheese, shredded
Shredded lettuce

In serving dish, layer beans, tomato, and onion. Top with Cheddar cheese and lettuce. Serve with oil-free tortilla chips.

Yield: about 2 cups dip

Nutrients per tablespoon:

Calories 20 Fat 0 g Carbohydrate 2 g Protein 1 g Sodium 53 mg Cholesterol 3 mg

Corn Salad

2 cups corn
¼ cup chopped red bell pepper
¼ cup chopped green bell pepper
¼ cup sliced scallions
½ cup nonfat red wine vinegar

Combine vegetables. Stir in dressing.

Yield: 6 servings

Nutrients per serving:

Calories 56 Fat 0 g Carbohydrate 14 g Protein 1 g Sodium 260 mg Cholesterol 0 mg

Family Reunion London Broil

¾ cup nonfat red wine
   vinegar dressing
3 cloves crushed garlic
¼ teaspoon cayenne pepper
1 large onion, finely
   chopped
1½ pounds round steak

Combine dressing, garlic, pepper, and onion. Pierce steak several times, place in shallow dish, and cover with marinade, turning once. Refrigerate one hour or more.

Marinated steak can be broiled, roasted, or cooked in closed barbecue pit over hot charcoal and basted with additional marinade.

Yield: 6 servings

Nutrients per serving:

Calories 157 Fat 4 g Carbohydrate 1 g Protein 29 g Sodium 52 mg Cholesterol 71 mg

Sweet Pepper Salad

3 yellow bell peppers,
   chopped
3 red bell peppers, chopped
¾ cup green onion slices
3 tablespoons chopped
   parsley
1½ cups nonfat Italian
   dressing

Mix bell peppers together; stir in onion and parsley. Top with dressing before serving.

Yield: 6 servings

Nutrients per serving:

Calories 50 Fat 0 g Carbohydrate 8 g Protein 1 g Sodium 583 mg Cholesterol 0 mg

Chunky Fruit Mousse

1 small package sugar-free
strawberry gelatin
¾ cup strawberry chunks
1 cup light whipped
topping

*Prepare gelatin per package
directions, chilling until slightly
thickened. Stir in fruit. Gently
fold in whipped topping. Chill
until firm.*

Yield: 6 servings

Nutrients per serving:

Calories 33 Fat 0 g Carbohydrate 7 g Protein 1 g Sodium 37 mg Cholesterol 0 mg

Berry Sparkling Slush

3 cups orange juice
½ cup lemon juice
2 cups ginger ale
1 (10-ounce) package frozen
raspberries, thawed
1 (10-ounce) package frozen
strawberries, thawed
2 cups seltzer water

*Combine all ingredients in
blender. Blend until smooth.*

Yield: about 10 cups

Nutrients per 1 cup:

Calories 75 Fat 0 g Carbohydrate 19 g Protein 0 g Sodium 4 mg Cholesterol 0 mg

*Lighter eating styles that are quite complementary
include vegetables combined with grain foods.*

Father's Day

King of the Feast

My father showed his love for me with Twinkies and Snowballs, Hostess cream-filled cupcakes and chocolate wheelies. He loved me with food, comforted me with food, and smothered me in food. When I fell off my bike and scraped my knee, he bought me a Happy Meal. When the nurse sent me home from school with the flu, he bought me chicken noodle soup and Chinese food. And the first time I left home, on an exchange trip to Europe, he bought me marzipan.

I learned of the world through the foods my father bought—foods of every nation. There were oranges from Florida, macadamia nuts from Hawaii, mangoes from the Caribbean, and chocolates from Italy. Every day there was something new to try—some new delicacy I had never heard of. And every day I traveled to a new place in the world through my father's kitchen.

When my father died, I was in a restaurant halfway across the country eating burritos and nachos. Suddenly, the man who had shown me the world from his kitchen was no longer present in the world I loved. He had shown me how to celebrate life in my appreciation of food, but never how to mourn it.

I mourn for all the things my father will miss in my life: He will never walk me down the aisle and give me away in marriage, never read a book I have written or congratulate me on some achievement well-earned, never hold my children in his arms, or travel the world with me. And I will never have the chance to feed him all the wonderful things I have learned to cook.

But when Father's Day comes around I remember him. And I prepare a feast in his honor—a gastronomic walk through the family photo album. I return to the foods of my childhood for one brief day, and I relish them. I buy chocolates and marzipan, Ding-Dongs and pizza, Chinese food and mangoes. And when the day is over, I close the album of my father's life and put away all the junk food and fast food and foreign food and snack food, and I return once again to a less eclectic way of eating.

But during those times in my life when I need my father to hold my hand and wipe away my tears, I go back to the remnants of my Father's Day feast, and I feast to remember.

Nisha N. Mohammed
Wantagh, NY

MAKE FATHER'S DAY A FAMILY AFFAIR. Gather all fathers and grand-fathers together at one home, and prepare a joint feast, making sure each one has a favorite item on the menu. It is a great time to relate "memories of father."

PLAN A SPECIAL OUTING WITH DAD, someplace the two of you used to go—a baseball game, the park, out for an ice-cream cone. Instead of a tie that you wear, get him a chocolate tie; it's a special day, so he can splurge a little on calories.

PREPARE A "THIS IS YOUR LIFE" FOR DAD. Track down 5 to 10 friends or coworkers from his past (this will take some deep investigative work on your part). Set up a schedule so each of them will phone him at a specific time on Father's Day. You pay the phone bill. It will be a day he'll never forget.

FATHER'S FEAST

Three-Bean Salad

❧ ❧ ❧

Summer Sizzling Steak
Spicy Chunks o' Barbecue
Roasted Corn

❧ ❧ ❧

Pineapple Strawberry Pie
Father's Day Coffee

❧ ❧ ❧

Three-Bean Salad

1 cup cooked green beans
1 cup cooked kidney beans
1 cup cooked garbanzo
   beans
½ cup chopped onions
½ cup chopped red pepper
1 cup balsamic vinegar
1 teaspoon black pepper

Combine all ingredients. Chill before serving.

Yield: 8 servings

Nutrients per serving:

Calories 72 Fat 0 g Carbohydrate 15 g Protein 4 g Sodium 112 mg Cholesterol 0 mg

Summer Sizzling Steak

½ cup white vinegar
¼ cup Worcestershire sauce
½ teaspoon garlic powder
1 teaspoon onion powder
1 pound round steak

Combine vinegar, Worcestershire sauce, and seasonings; mix well. With a fork, pierce steak in several places. Place steak in a shallow dish, and cover with marinade, turning once. Refrigerate for one hour or longer. Marinated steak can be broiled or grilled.

Yield: 4 servings

Nutrients per serving:

Calories 159 Fat 4 g Carbohydrate 1 g Protein 27 g Sodium 101 mg Cholesterol 71 mg

Spicy Chunks o' Barbecue

1 (16-ounce) can crushed tomatoes
¼ cup honey
2 tablespoons vinegar
¼ teaspoon garlic powder
½ teaspoon onion powder

Combine all ingredients. Mix well. Use to baste meats on the grill or in the oven; barbecue sauce can also be served at the table.

Yield: about 2½ cups

Nutrients per tablespoon:

Calories 10 Fat 0 g Carbohydrate 2 g Protein 0 g Sodium 17 mg Cholesterol 0 mg

Roasted Corn

4 ears corn
¼ cup diet margarine
1 tablespoon chopped parsley
1 tablespoon black pepper

Clean corn; set aside. Melt margarine; stir in seasonings. Spread 1 tablespoon mixture on each ear of corn. Wrap corn in foil. Roast over hot charcoal until tender.

Yield: 4 servings

Nutrients per ear of corn:

Calories 133 Fat 7 g Carbohydrate 19 g Protein 3 g Sodium 149 mg Cholesterol 0 mg

Everyone's calorie needs differ depending on his body size and activity level.

Pineapple Strawberry Pie

1 (15-ounce) can crushed
   pineapple
1 pint strawberries, coarsely
   chopped
1 (8-ounce) container
   whipped topping
1 (8-inch) graham cracker
   crust

*Fold fruit into whipped topping;
pour into crust. Freeze until firm.
Allow to thaw slightly at room
temperature before serving.*

Yield: 8 servings

Nutrients per serving:

Calories 217 Fat 8 g Carbohydrate 37 g Protein 1 g Sodium 185 mg Cholesterol 0 mg

Father's Day Coffee

1 quart coffee, cooled
1 quart water
½ cup chocolate syrup
Powdered sugar substitute
   to taste

*For each serving, place two ice
cubes in a 10-ounce glass. Add ½
cup coffee, ½ cup water, and 1
tablespoon chocolate syrup. Mix
well. Serve with powdered sugar
substitute. Serve over ice.*

Yield: 8 (1-cup) servings

Nutrients per 1 cup serving:

Calories 25 Fat 0 g Carbohydrate 6 g Protein 0 g Sodium 10 mg Cholesterol 0 mg

Star Gazing

The Starry Night Sky

The night sky holds romance, mystery, comfort. Anyone who has been *in love* knows what I mean. There is something beautiful about a night sky full of stars with a warm wind blowing. Not necessarily *in love* with a person. Perhaps *in love* with nature, with life. But *in love*. Love enhances one's experience of a starry night sky.

One of my most vivid experiences with the night sky and with love was my first date with a "special" guy. We were in college. That meant that we had time to spend doing anything, everything. A time to just enjoy. He planned our first date. It started with a spaghetti dinner (probably Ragu, but it was very nice to have *him* cook *me* dinner). Then off to a fair held down by the river. Hand in hand, we went around to the different booths, sampling what we could and signing up for free giveaways. After awhile, he must have read my mind for he said he wanted to take me to a "special spot." Alone at last.

His special spot was a beautiful little place in the country about 30 minutes away. We tucked his car away from the highway and took a blanket out into a field. Surrounded by wheat and covered by stars, we weren't really alone. There was so much beauty, so much to take in. "What's that one, over there, over that oak?" "Pleiades," he responded. "The cluster is also known as the Seven Sisters and looks like a sideways question mark." What are the sisters asking me? Do they wonder if I am in love? And just who am I in love with? The night and all of its mystery and magic—or this guy sitting here about to kiss me? Perhaps it is a combination.

I learned about stars that night, something about love, a lot about myself. Being out in nature, being a part of it, sets me free. When I look at a starry night sky, I listen for my Pleiades and the probing questions they might ask. They often beckon me to open my eyes to the grandeur of their home high above me. They help me soar while also grounding me on my tiny planet. I like to think that the night sky is my first love, but in close competition with that guy who introduced me to the beauty and mystery of the stars. For you see, that guy has now become my husband.

Dawn Richardson
Memphis, TN

To truly enjoy the night sky, LEARN ABOUT THE STARS AND VARI-OUS FORMATIONS. A good way to do this is to visit a planetarium near you to get a close up view of the heavens with an expert pointing out highlights. Most cities have a museum that has a planetarium. It's an enjoyable way to spend a few hours.

A SIMPLE GUIDEBOOK TO THE STARS is *The Night Sky: A Guide to the Stars*, published by Running Press Gem. A more detailed book, giving information on galaxies, telescope usage, etc., is *Night Watch: An Equinox Guide To Viewing the Universe*, published by Camden House. Guidebooks give information on particular events that might be of interest, such as meteor showers, and tell you when to look for them.

On a starry night, DRIVE AT LEAST 30 MILES OUTSIDE A CITY. The lights from the city prevent you from seeing the best show. Take along a pair of binoculars to try to get a glimpse of the rings of Saturn.

DINNER UNDER THE STARS

Chili Popcorn
Garden Green Salad

🦌 🦌 🦌

Tasty Chillin' Beef
Corny Bites

🦌 🦌 🦌

Melon-Berry Finale
Tangy Sunshine Punch

🦌 🦌 🦌

Chili Popcorn

4 cups popped popcorn
1 teaspoon chili powder
2 tablespoons Parmesan
cheese

*Mix popcorn with chili powder
and cheese. Toss well.*

Yield: 4 (1-cup) servings

Nutrients per serving:

Calories 38 Fat 1 g Carbohydrate 5 g Protein 1 g Sodium 64 mg Cholesterol 4 mg

Garden Green Salad

2 cups torn romaine lettuce
2 cups torn Bibb lettuce
2 cups torn iceberg lettuce
2 cups torn spinach
Nonfat dressing

*Toss greens together. Serve with
choice of nonfat dressings.*

Yield: about 8 servings

Nutrients per serving:

Calories 25 Fat 0 g Carbohydrate 5 g Protein 1 g Sodium 10 mg Cholesterol 0 mg

*Vary food textures in each meal; serve something
crunchy, smooth, and crisp together.*

Tasty Chillin' Beef

1 pound top round steak
1 cup red wine vinegar
1 teaspoon cracked black
  pepper
1 tablespoon lemon juice

Cut steak into pieces that are about 2 x 4 inches. Combine vinegar with pepper and lemon juice. Marinate beef pieces in vinegar mixture several hours or overnight. Broil or grill steak pieces; serve cold in sandwiches.

Yield: 4 servings

Nutrients per serving:

Calories 153 Fat 4 g Carbohydrate 0 g Protein 27 g Sodium 52 mg Cholesterol 71 mg

Corny Bites

2 cups cooked corn
¼ cup chopped chives
½ cup chopped onion
¼ cup chopped parsley
½ cup nonfat Italian
  dressing

Combine first 4 ingredients. Stir in dressing.

Yield: about 6 servings

Nutrients per serving:

Calories 55 Fat 0 g Carbohydrate 14 g Protein 1 g Sodium 260 mg Cholesterol 0 mg

Melon-Berry Finale

½ medium honeydew
   melon, cubed
8 medium strawberries,
   halved
2 cups diced watermelon

*Combine fruit; toss well. Chill
before serving.*

Yield: about 6 servings

Nutrients per serving:

Calories 63 Fat 0 g Carbohydrate 15 g Protein 1 g Sodium 10 g Cholesterol 0 mg

Tangy Sunshine Punch

3 cups grapefruit juice
1 cup lemon juice
2 cups ginger ale
1½ cups pineapple juice
1 cup water

*Combine all ingredients. Chill
before serving.*

Yield: 8½ cups

Nutrients per cup:

Calories 84 Fat 0 g Carbohydrate 22 g Protein 0 g Sodium 6 g Cholesterol 0 mg

Kid's Birthday

Nirvana in the Backyard

Starlight mingled with porch light best describes my 10th birthday experience. Instead of inviting friends over for the usual cake and ice cream, Mom said my best friend and I could camp out. We spent all day in the backyard preparing for that adventure. We dragged the picnic table off the patio and found just the right spot for it. Draped with an old quilt, the table served as our tent. Mom packed the birthday cake left over from dinner and enough snacks for a summer's worth of sleepovers. She also left the door unlocked "just in case." As dusk settled, we galloped around the yard, our bare feet tickled by the damp, freshly mowed grass. This frenzied, zigzagging dance yielded enough fireflies to fill our mayonnaise jars. They cast a haunting glow under the "picnic" tent that seemed perfect for telling secrets and stories. This was a 10-year-old's nirvana. (Keep in mind, I grew up before cable TV and Nintendo.)

Years later my niece turned 10, so I asked her and her 8-year-old sister to go camping to celebrate the event. We spent the better part of the day hiking and searching for just the right spot to pitch our tents. I wrestled with a tangle of nylon and unwieldy aluminum stakes and thought it a shame I couldn't picnic on this when camping was over. The sun began to tease us with shafts of light here and there before it finally faded behind the trees. A familiar feeling of pure, intoxicating bliss washed over me as adult frustrations and worries disappeared. Spitting sparks in the crisp night air, the campfire cast haunting shadows in a frenzied, zigzagging dance on the trees. Pretty soon, stories and secrets spilled out, and I, too, was 10 years old again. That night, my nieces had no need for cable TV and Nintendo either.

Dawn Pradat
Birmingham, AL

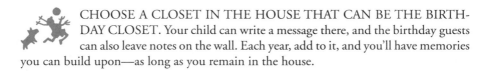 CHOOSE A CLOSET IN THE HOUSE THAT CAN BE THE BIRTH-DAY CLOSET. Your child can write a message there, and the birthday guests can also leave notes on the wall. Each year, add to it, and you'll have memories you can build upon—as long as you remain in the house.

HAVE A BACKWARDS PARTY. Invitations should be written backwards (on the inside), and everyone arrives dressed with clothes on backwards. Birthday favors are hats with each child's name spelled backwards, and it has to be worn in the same manner. Eat under a large table with everyone facing the wall and eating with the opposite end of his utensils. Play volleyball with everyone facing away from the net. *.yad nuf A*

B I R T H D A Y   B O N A N Z A

Garlic Bread
Meatless Antipasto

🍒 🍒 🍒

Luncheon Meat Rollups
Melon Cube Toss

🍒 🍒 🍒

Banana Applesauce Cake
Cool 'n' Creamy Lemon-Lime Treat

🍒 🍒 🍒

Garlic Bread

1 (1-pound) loaf Italian
   bread
¼ cup diet margarine
1 teaspoon garlic powder
1 teaspoon onion powder

Preheat oven to 400°. Melt margarine over low heat; stir in seasoning. Slice Italian bread lengthwise down center. Drizzle margarine mixture down center cut in bread. Heat bread in oven approximately 5 minutes or until crispy. Serve warm.

Yield: 15 slices

Nutrients per slice:

Calories 110 Fat 6 g Carbohydrate 17 g Protein 3 g Sodium 250 mg Cholesterol 0 mg

Meatless Antipasto

4 tomatoes, cut into wedges
2 zucchini, cut into sticks
2 cucumbers, cut into
   wedges
2 carrots, cut into sticks
Light Italian dressing
   (optional)

Arrange all ingredients in above order on a serving tray. Serve with light Italian dressing, if desired.

Yield: 12 servings

Nutrients per serving:

Calories 34 Fat 0 g Carbohydrate 8 g Protein 1 g Sodium 10 g Cholesterol 0 mg

Luncheon Meat Rollups

4 slices turkey salami
4 slices turkey bologna
4 slices turkey ham
12 slices light cheese

For each rollup, place one slice of cheese on a luncheon meat slice. Roll and place seam-side down on serving platter.

Yield: 12 rollups

Nutrients per rollup (including cheese):

With turkey salami: Calories 80 Fat 5 g Carbohydrate 4 g Protein 8 g Sodium 323 mg Cholesterol 28 mg

With turkey bologna: Calories 100 Fat 7 g Carbohydrate 4 g Protein 6 g Sodium 516 mg Cholesterol 27 mg

With turkey ham: Calories 73 Fat 4 g Carbohydrate 3 g Protein 9 g Sodium 576 mg Cholesterol 25 mg

Melon Cube Toss

3 cups watermelon cubes
1½ cups cantaloupe cubes
1½ cups honeydew melon cubes
¾ cup raisins
Powdered sugar

Combine melon cubes; stir in raisins. Sprinkle with powdered sugar before serving.

Yield: 12 servings

Nutrients per serving:

Calories 55 Fat 0 g Carbohydrate 14 g Protein 0 g Sodium 15 mg Cholesterol 0 mg

For variety, fruit can be served as a side dish instead of a vegetable.

Banana Applesauce Cake

¾ cup applesauce
¼ cup vegetable oil
1¼ cups sugar
2 eggs
6 ripe bananas, mashed
2 teaspoons vanilla extract
4 cups flour, sifted
1 teaspoon baking soda

Preheat oven to 325°. Combine applesauce, oil, sugar, and eggs. Add bananas and vanilla; set aside. Combine flour and baking soda; gradually stir into applesauce mixture. Beat for 2 minutes. Pour into greased tube pan, and bake for 1½ hours or until inserted toothpick comes out clean.

Yield: 12 servings

Nutrients per serving:
Calories 300 Fat 6 g Carbohydrate 56 g Protein 5 g Sodium 46 g Cholesterol 35 mg

Cool 'n' Creamy Lemon-Lime Treat

½ cup lemon juice
½ cup lime juice
2 quarts water
2 cups lime sherbet, slightly softened
2 cups diet lemon-lime flavored soda

Combine all ingredients; mix well. Serve immediately.

Yield: 12 (1-cup) servings

Nutrients per cup:
Calories 38 Fat 0 g Carbohydrate 8 g Protein 0 g Sodium 11 mg Cholesterol 2 mg

House or Apartment Hunting

... House or Apartment Hunting

The Residence "Hunt"

. . . .

At first glance, as I looked out into the city, I couldn't exactly see all the apartment buildings camouflaged against parking garages, leaning against convenient stores, and lurking behind mall strips. But I knew the home for me was out there, and I was going to find it. It was simply a matter of stalking in the right direction because although it would hide, I knew it certainly could not run. Armed with tape measure, clipboard, and checkbook, I lurched into the streets. It was open season, and I was apartment hunting.

I had already decided to bypass all landlords knowing that their office hours and search for spare keys would slow me down, sacrificing the surprise of the attack. So when I finally cornered a building with potential, I glared at it from the street (showing it just exactly who was in control), then marched up the front steps and walked right in.

Once it caught sight of my checkbook, it shivered with fear, even spraying me with its nasty foyer scent, hoping for a retreat. But to no avail. I began knocking on door after door, waiting for someone to open up so I could get a good look at its innards. TVs and radios blared from behind closed doors, but no one answered until, at the end of a long hallway, I must have found the heart, a weak spot, the perfect chance for the kill...a door cracked open.

Slowly I reeled out the tape measure (my collapsible Winchester), scribbled the address on the clipboard, and peered inside. It was empty. A vacancy. There it was—caught, trapped, crouched frozen in my headlights. "Ha ha," I yelled (and it echoed), "you're finished!" As I walked its rooms, it groaned with the ache of surrender.

After the task of showing licenses, tagging, and registration came the gory mess of stripping and tanning. Every corner was rid of any past identity and sterilized beyond recognition.

When the hunt was over and my apartment was under complete submission, I wondered why I never took it to a taxidermist. I mean, what else do we hunt, besides a house or apartment, that we don't eventually stuff and mount—or immediately stuff and eat?

Jennifer Wolfe
St. Louis, MO

109

Working with a real estate broker is helpful to save you lots of legwork and aggravation. ASK IF THEY CAN GIVE YOU 10 PLACES TO DRIVE BY first, so you can narrow down the process. Just remember that first impressions may be wrong. That cold-looking monster of a house or apartment that needs painting may be warm and cozy and newly renovated to your liking on the inside.

TAKE ALONG AN INSTANT CAMERA to take outside shots, so you have something to refer to. As you go through the house or apartment, make notes on the back of the photo of things you liked. If you don't use a process like this, everything will blur together.

When the papers are signed, PLAN A MOVE IN PARTY OR A PAINTING PARTY. This gives your friends a chance to see your new abode—and also helps you out with some "inexpensive labor."

AFTER THE HUNT

Cream Cheese Canapé Sandwiches
Green Bean and Mushroom Vinaigrette

❦ ❦ ❦

Creamy Chicken Salad
Zesty Beans and Peppers

❦ ❦ ❦

Sunset Fruit Medley
Lemony Iced Tea

❦ ❦ ❦

Cream Cheese Canapé Sandwiches

1 (8-ounce) container
   nonfat cream cheese
1 teaspoon garlic powder
1 teaspoon onion powder
1 tablespoon chopped
   chives
32 fat-free cracked-pepper
   crackers

Soften cream cheese at room temperature. Stir in spices; blend well. For each canapé, spread 1 tablespoon of mixture on a cracker, and top with another cracker.

Yield: 16 sandwich canapés.

Nutrients per canapé:

Calories 31 Fat 0 g Carbohydrate 5 g Protein 3 g Sodium 114 g Cholesterol 2 mg

Green Bean and Mushroom Vinaigrette

½ pound green beans
1½ cups sliced mushrooms
½ cup green onion slices
1 (8-ounce) bottle oil-free
   Italian dressing

Steam vegetables just until tender. Mix vegetables with dressing. Marinate one hour or longer.

Yield: 6 servings

Nutrients per serving:

Calories 20 Fat 0 g Carbohydrate 5 g Protein 0 g Sodium 600 mg Cholesterol 0 mg

Creamy Chicken Salad

12 ounces cooked, skinned chicken breast, diced
 1 cup chopped celery
 ½ cup chopped onion
 ½ cup nonfat mayonnaise
 ¼ cup nonfat yogurt
 1 teaspoon black pepper
 ¼ cup red bell pepper

Combine all ingredients. Chill before serving.

Yield: 4 servings

Nutrients per serving:

Calories 199 Fat 3 g Carbohydrate 12 g Protein 29 g Sodium 535 mg Cholesterol 74 mg

Zesty Beans and Peppers

2 cups cooked red kidney beans
2 medium green bell peppers, chopped
1 medium onion, chopped
1 cup bottle oil-free Italian dressing

Mix vegetables together. Pour dressing over vegetables; mix well.

Yield: 4 servings

Nutrients per serving:

Calories 55 Fat 0 g Carbohydrate 14 g Protein 2 g Sodium 904 mg Cholesterol 0 mg

Sunset Fruit Medley

2 cups watermelon balls
2 cups cantaloupe balls
2 cups honeydew melon
  balls
1 tablespoon powdered
  sugar

Combine fruit together. Sprinkle with powdered sugar. Serve immediately.

Yield: 6 servings

Nutrients per serving:

Calories 50 Fat 0 g Carbohydrate 12 Protein 1 g Sodium 30 mg Cholesterol 0 mg

Lemony Iced Tea

3 quarts water
4 tea bags
¾ cup lemon juice
  Sugar or sweetener to taste

Boil water, and pour over tea bags in heat-resistant pitcher; steep for 5 minutes. Remove tea bags; add lemon juice. Chill and serve over ice. Sweeten with sugar to taste.

Yield: about 12 cups

Nutrients per cup:

Calories 4 Fat 0 g Carbohydrate 1 g Protein 0 g Sodium 0 mg Cholesterol 0 mg

Nothing sweetens the end of a meal better than a generous serving of seasonal fresh fruit!

Canoeing

Wet Adventure on a Lazy River

We were all first-time canoers beginning a four-hour journey down the Little Cahaba River. My husband and I set out with two other couples to Centreville, Alabama, for a fun-filled afternoon canoeing trip that taught all of us a great deal about teamwork, marriage, and maintaining a sense of humor. Patience wore thin and relationships were tested, but when the day ended we could only remember the best parts of our trip.

After donning our life jackets and garnering a few basic instructions from the folks at Bulldog Bend Canoeing Park, we timidly began our big adventure. Water was low on the river that day, which we thought would be good for beginners; however, maneuvering the rocks became the main focus of our attention. Oftentimes, we got out of our canoes to drag them to deeper water. On occasion, the water deepened, and that gentle friendly river turned into a swift-moving foe, spilling us into the cold water when we misjudged our approach. Each couple had its turn at the fun, with heated, but well-meant, instructions bellowed often: "Watch out for that rock," "Work with me on this turn," and "Next time, let's hit the small rapids head on instead of sideways." It was easy for the other couples to snicker when the instructions weren't targeted at them. Too often the inexperience lost, and the river won the battle between oar and rock.

Even though we were novices, we came prepared for mishaps and secured our food and drinks in coolers that we tied to the canoes. After a few hours of paddling, we pulled to the riverbank to share our feast. Food always tastes great when you're outdoors and tired from physical activity. As we nibbled on chicken salad sandwiches, fresh fruit, chocolate cookies, and liquid refreshments, we laughed about missed rapids and teased about poor paddling skills. Of course, each of us thought we were the only one in our canoe who knew what he (or she) was doing.

When our journey ended, we had sore muscles, a bruise or two, and a few humbled egos. We shared laughter, good food, and most importantly, an experience that created warm memories that all of us can recall for years to come. And will we go canoeing soon again? Why not! We're no longer novices.

Vicki Weathers
Birmingham, AL

For clean waters, high bluffs, wooded hillsides, and seasonal wildflowers, PADDLE THE BUFFALO NATIONAL RIVER, with national park headquarters in Harrison, Arkansas. The canoeing groups are well organized along the river, and there are many slow-moving river sections, which is a great help to novices. For details, call (501) 741-5443.

 FOR AN INTERMEDIATE-LEVEL RIVER, travel to western Wyoming near Jackson. Not only is this area known for great skiing, but canoeing should not be ignored here as well. The Snake River Kayak and Canoe School has some great planned trips; call (307) 733-3127.

 In Tennessee, near Chattanooga, the Ocoee River, with intermediate and upper-level rapids, PROVIDES A GREAT SPOT FOR CANOEING AND RAFTING. Contact: Outdoor Adventure Rafting, 1-800-627-7636; Nantahala Outdoor Center, 1-800-232-7238; or Outland Expeditions, 1-800-827-1442.

 A LARGE PLASTIC, EMPTY PAINT CONTAINER WITH A TIGHT-FITTING LID provides a perfect storage area for all your items (lunch, sunglasses, wallets, etc.) while canoeing. Fill it, make sure the lid is secure, and tie it to the canoe. If you tip over, everything will stay dry (except you) and not be floating down the river.

TIPOVER PICNIC

Corn Relish Topping
Chick Pea Salad

❧ ❧ ❧

Deep Sea Lobster Salad
Rancher's Beans and Corn

❧ ❧ ❧

Peachy Blueberry Delight
Orange Cube Spritzer

❧ ❧ ❧

Corn Relish Topping

1 cup corn
½ teaspoon celery seed
½ teaspoon mustard seed
1 green bell pepper, chopped
1 small onion, chopped
1 medium pimiento
½ cup cider vinegar
1 tablespoon honey

Combine all ingredients. Mix well. Use as a topping for salads or as a spread on hot dogs and hamburgers.

Yield: about 3 cups

Nutrients per tablespoon:

Calories 7 Fat 0 g Carbohydrate 2 g Protein 0 g Sodium 0 mg Cholesterol 0 mg

Chick Pea Salad

¼ cup vinegar
1 tablespoon olive oil
1 tablespoon minced garlic
1½ cups cooked chick peas
¼ cup chopped onion
¼ cup chopped celery

Mix vinegar, olive oil and garlic together; set aside. Combine peas and vegetables, mix well. Stir in vinegar and oil mixture. Serve at room temperature.

Yield: 8 servings

Nutrients per serving:

Calories 69 Fat 3 g Carbohydrate 9 g Protein 2 g Sodium 2 mg Cholesterol 0 mg

Deep Sea Lobster Salad

1 pound imitation lobster
  chunks
2 tomatoes, cut into wedges
½ cup chopped celery
2 cups spinach, torn
½ cup red wine vinegar
1 tablespoon lemon juice

Combine all ingredients. Chill
before serving.

Yield: 4 servings

Nutrients per serving:

Calories 145 Fat 2 g Carbohydrate 15 g Protein 18 g Sodium 595 mg Cholesterol 31 mg

Rancher's Beans and Corn

1 cup red kidney beans
1 cup cooked corn
1 cup chopped green bell
  pepper
1 (8-ounce) bottle nonfat
  ranch dressing
½ teaspoon chili powder

Mix vegetables together; stir in
dressing. Sprinkle with chili
powder, and stir lightly. (Top
with Corn Relish Topping, if
desired.)

Yield: 6 servings

Nutrients per serving:

Calories 102 Fat 0 g Carbohydrate 24 g Protein 2 g Sodium 415 mg Cholesterol 0 mg

*Enjoy your summer fun with high-energy, low-fat
eating styles.*

Peachy Blueberry Delight

4 large peaches, diced
2 cups blueberries
¼ cup sugar
¼ cup brown sugar
2 teaspoons cinnamon

Combine peaches and blueberries. Mix sugars and cinnamon together; stir into fruit. Refrigerate several hours.

Yield: 6 servings

Nutrients per serving:

Calories 118 Fat 0 g Carbohydrate 32 g Protein 1 g Sodium 3 mg Cholesterol 0 mg

Orange Cube Spritzer

1 envelope plain gelatin
1 cup water
1 (6-ounce) can frozen orange juice
1 (2-liter) bottle seltzer water

Soften gelatin in 1 cup water in a small saucepan (about 5 minutes); dissolve gelatin over low heat, stirring constantly. Remove from heat; add orange juice concentrate, and mix well. Lightly coat ice cube trays with nonstick spray. Pour mixture into trays. Cover and freeze.
Pour seltzer into traveling containers, add cubes.

Yield: about 8 cups

Nutrients per 1 cup:

Calories 50 Fat 0 g Carbohydrate 12 g Protein 0 g Sodium 0 mg Cholesterol 0 mg

Weekend at Grandma's

Coming Home To Eat

. . . .

To remember summers at Grandma and Papa's old place is to formulate a wealth of associations that coalesce around the idea of coming home to eat. Right down from their house is an even older place—a family place poised between cottonfields and cow pastures, with a dinner bell in the yard that used to ring people in—bring them home to eat. Most of my images of long weekends at Grandma and Papa's, oddly enough, have to do with events surrounding the meal.

Shucking corn, shelling peas, snapping beans on the back porch in the twilight. Soft conversation with the murmur of the T.V. coming out from the living room. Cutting a watermelon or churning peach ice cream in the shade of the water oak in the backyard. Slicing plump, juicy tomatoes picked from the vine you tied to the stake. Walking between rows under the Southern sun— weeding. Turning over the soil. Planting.

Modern culture has removed us from processes that are a part of our history—part of our story. In the name of convenience, it is arranged for us to receive the benefits of a process of which we no longer have to be a part. And there's no denying the convenience of frozen foods and microwaves. But I miss the feel of earth—the sun on my back—miss talking to Papa about whether we'll have enough rain or too much and have that be more than a matter of convenience or inconvenience. I miss the quiet times of communion on the back porch—taking turns on the crank of the ice-cream churn with aunts and uncles and cousins and brothers and sisters and parents and grandparents in the shade of a tree.

Interconnectedness is not an experience common and treasured. Interdependence is not sought and celebrated. But I know that by the time we would get around to eating at Grandma and Papa's, I was always full—full of the kind of nourishment you can't buy and you can't consume. Full of life. And I know that as housing developments encroach on cottonfields, and cow pastures are sold, and families move, and dinner bells aren't used anymore, there is a hunger—growing.

Plant a tomato. Shuck corn with someone. You wash, I'll dry. Feed your soul.

John Ballenger
Laurens, SC

MAKE ONE WEEKEND MEAL TOGETHER AN OLD-FASHIONED SUPPER—even if Grandma or Papa now live in an apartment. Buy the fresh produce; make a production out of preparing a good country meal. It will bring back good memories for all of you. Ask them to get out the old photos, and reminisce about life when they were growing up. You can learn a lot from those experiences.

SURPRISE YOUR GRANDPARENTS WITH THIS PICNIC SUPPER for your first meal together when you arrive. You can prepare everything ahead of time and do the grilling once you arrive. As folks get older, it's harder for them to entertain guests; if you have this meal ready to go it will be a big help for them

---

S U R P R I S E   S U P P E R

Stuffed Celery Sticks
Vegetable Kebabs

🍎 🍎 🍎

Cheddary Potatoes
Land and Sea Kebabs

🍎 🍎 🍎

Summertime Fruit Salad
Citrus Iced Tea

🍎 🍎 🍎

Stuffed Celery Sticks

1 bunch celery
2 cups nonfat cream cheese
½ teaspoon hot sauce
2 tablespoons cracked
   pepper

Remove tops from celery; cut
individual stalks into thirds.
Blend cream cheese and hot
sauce together; stir in pepper.
Spread mixture into celery pieces.

Yield: 24 stuffed celery pieces

Nutrients per 3 pieces:

Calories 78 Fat 0 g Carbohydrate 7 g Protein 11 g Sodium 355 mg Cholesterol 8 mg

Vegetable Kebabs

1 medium onion, cut into
   chunks
½ cup eggplant cubes
1 medium-size red bell
   pepper, cut into chunks
1 medium-size green bell
   pepper, cut into chunks
1 tablespoon olive oil

Alternate vegetables on skewer;
brush lightly with olive oil. Grill
skewered vegetables directly on
rack over medium hot coals; turn
once and continue grilling to
desired tenderness.

Yield: about 4 (½-cup) servings

Nutrients per serving:

Calories 64 Fat 4 g Carbohydrate 6 g Protein 0 g Sodium 2 mg Cholesterol 0 mg

Cheddary Potatoes

4 medium potatoes
¼ cup shredded reduced-fat Cheddar cheese
¼ cup chives
1 teaspoon black pepper

Pierce potatoes; microwave in skin until fork tender. Toss cheese, chives, and black pepper together. Partially split open potatoes lengthwise; fill each with one-fourth the cheese mixture. Close potatoes; wrap in foil, and heat over hot charcoals until cheese melts, about 5 minutes.

Yield: 4 servings

Nutrients per potato:

Calories 130 Fat 1 g Carbohydrate 23 g Protein 5 g Sodium 60 mg Cholesterol 5 mg

Land and Sea Kebabs

½ pound top round eye roast, cut into chunks
1 cup red wine vinegar fat-free dressing
½ pound shrimp

Marinate roast chunks in dressing one hour or longer; pan grill until brown. Alternate roast chunks with shrimp on skewer; grill until shrimp is opaque, brushing with dressing while grilling.

Yield: 4 servings

Nutrients per serving:

Calories 142 Fat 3 g Carbohydrate 6 g Protein 23 g Sodium 900 mg Cholesterol 109 mg

Summertime Fruit Salad

8 medium strawberries, halved
2 medium peaches, cubed
1 cup blueberries
Powdered sugar

Toss fruits together; sprinkle with sugar.

Yield: about 6 (½-cup) servings

Nutrients per serving:

Calories 35 Fat 0 g Carbohydrate 8 g Protein 0 g Sodium 0 g Cholesterol 0 g

Citrus Iced Tea

1 quart boiling water
4 tea bags
1½ quarts cold water
½ cup orange juice
½ cup lemon juice
Sugar substitute to taste

Pour boiling water over tea bags in heat-resistant pitcher; allow tea to steep for 5 minutes. Add cold water and juices; chill thoroughly. Sweeten to taste as desired with sugar substitute.

Yield: about 11 cups

Nutrients per cup:

Calories 35 Fat 0 g Carbohydrate 8 g Protein 0 g Sodium 0 mg Cholesterol 0 mg

With take-along food, meals on the road are your choice for health-conscious living.

Drive-In Movies

Drive-In Groovy

I have always said—or, at least, often thought—that a person can never *truly* understand something unless he has actually experienced it. One such something is a drive-in movie in Southern summertime.

For those who know what I'm talking about, I am sure that the words I just uttered caused instant flashbacks. You can again feel the dampness of your hair, which will never fully dry, from the humid night air. The smell of bug spray, which is the true and unromanticized smell of Southern summer, is invading your nose. And suddenly, after all this time, you and I are nine years old again, and we are sitting on the tailgate of a metallic cherry Chevrolet Silverado pick-up truck. Our legs, with bandaids crisscrossed here and there, are dangling as we gaze expectantly at the gargantuan screen of the drive-in movie.

Then, like magic (for everything at 9 is still magical), a single beam of light shoots across the rat maze parking log and animates the screen. And there they are—tap dancing and singing like no other refreshments could then or have since—the pronto pup, the popcorn, the Coke, and the candy. This was the signal, the sign from the theatrical gods. The cartoon that said to every kid on every tailgate across that parking lot, "EAT! EAT!" After racing to the concession booth, we would order: a large Coke, Sugar Babies, and a large popcorn with extra butter, of course. Please and thank you very much, ma'am.

I'm still not sure if it was all that food that we ate, but we always fell asleep before the movie ended. It might have been the heat. Southern heat will do that to you. Really. That's the thing. People can never truly understand what they have not experienced.

Leigh Ann McIntosh
Memphis, TN

YOU MAY THINK THAT DRIVE-IN MOVIES HAVE GONE THE WAY of Ozzie and Harriet, but there are still many scattered around the country. The experience is well worth the search.

 SPRING AND SUMMER MAY BE THE BEST TIMES to enjoy the drive-in, but some establishments operate year-round by supplying heaters to keep you warm during colder weather.

MOVIE MUNCHIES

Crabmeat Dip
Green Bean Salad

❦ ❦ ❦

Shrimp 'n' Rice Salad
Corn Medley

❦ ❦ ❦

Applesauce Muffins
Sparkling Quencher

❦ ❦ ❦

Crabmeat Dip

1 (8-ounce) package nonfat
   cream cheese
2 tablespoons skim milk
1 (7-ounce) can crabmeat,
   drained and rinsed
2 teaspoons lemon juice

Combine all ingredients; mix well. Serve dip with crackers

Yield: about 2 cups

Nutrients per 1 tablespoon:

Calories 20 Fat 0 g Carbohydrate 1 g Protein 4 g Sodium 33 mg Cholesterol 13 mg

Green Bean Salad

1 pound green beans,
   cooked
2 medium tomatoes,
   chopped
¼ cup chopped red onion
1 cup oil-free Italian
   dressing

Combine the first 3 ingredients; mix well. Add dressing, and toss together. Chill several hours before serving.

Yield: 4 servings

Nutrients per serving:

Calories 35 Fat 0 g Carbohydrate 8 g Protein 1 g Sodium 604 mg Cholesterol 0 mg

Shrimp 'n' Rice Salad

1 pound shrimp, cooked
3 cups cooked rice
¼ cup chopped onion
1 cup nonfat mayonnaise

Peel and devein shrimp; coarsely chop into bite-size pieces. Combine shrimp, rice, and onion. Moisten mixture with mayonnaise. Refrigerate before serving.

Yield: 4 servings

Nutrients per serving:

Calories 300 Fat 2 g Carbohydrate 39 g Protein 24 g Sodium 938 mg Cholesterol 160 mg

Corn Medley

1½ cups corn
½ cup chopped red bell pepper
¼ cup chopped red onion
2 tablespoons chopped green bell pepper
Nonfat dressing

Combine all ingredients. Serve with nonfat dressing.

Yield: 4 servings

Nutrients per serving:

Calories 64 Fat 1 g Carbohydrate 14 g Protein 2 g Sodium 11 mg Cholesterol 0 mg

Applesauce Muffins

2 cups flour
⅓ cup sugar
2 teaspoons baking powder
⅔ cup applesauce
½ cup skim milk

Preheat oven to 400°. Combine dry ingredients. Add applesauce and milk; mix just until moistened. Spoon into nonstick muffin pan, filling each cup about two-thirds full. Bake 20 to 25 minutes or until lightly brown.

Yield: 1 dozen muffins

Nutrients per muffin:

Calories 85 Fat 0 g Carbohydrate 18 g Protein 2 g Sodium 60 mg Cholesterol 0 mg

Sparkling Quencher

1 (6-ounce) can frozen
  limeade
4 cups cold water
2 cups cranberry juice
  cocktail
2 cups diet lemon-lime soda

Combine limeade, water, and cranberry juice; add soda just before serving.

Yield: 10 (6-ounce) servings

Nutrients per serving:

Calories 68 Fat 0 g Carbohydrates 17 Protein 0 g Sodium 0 mg Cholesterol 0 mg

Eat light at night. Make your last meal of the day one that will not show on you.

Pool Party

Cooling Off the Summer Daze

Summer in Phoenix, Arizona, lasts for about 150 days. Usually the gang would meander to my house to partake of the coolness of the pool. However, many days I spent alone on my back in the pool, floating on a raft and dreaming with a glass of lemonade in one hand and a tennis ball in the other. I'd toss the tennis ball high in the air and paddle aimlessly over to where it splashed in the water, repeating the same motion as my skin crispened and stung, until I finally had to throw myself in. I could almost feel the steam rise as I splashed down.

In my pool days, I listened to a tiny radio, turned up to full volume. Summer was the time for baseball. For me, that meant the Los Angeles Dodgers. Actually going to a game would have been too much effort; I preferred to let my imagination wander around the hallowed grounds of Dodger Stadium, making the feats seem more spectacular, the great plays even greater than they actually were. Who knows whether the games I actually listened to even took place? Inning by inning, pitch by pitch, they were re-created in my sun-baked imagination in that kidney-shaped Phoenix pool, several hundred miles away. The most transcendent moments came when Dodger announcer Vin Scully would intone his home run call: "There's a high fly ball to deep left-center field. Back goes Geronimo, a waaaaay back, to the wall, it's gone! Home run Garvey!" As the balls sailed out of the stadium, it was as though I was riding on their seams, spinning into an eternal home-run trot, until the sun would make me blister and I once again would have to plunge myself into the reality of my backyard pool.

Neal Pollack
Chicago, Il

A SUCCESSFUL POOL PARTY must have beach ball, an umbrella, insect repellant, suntan lotion, and loads of music.

 WHEN THE GANG DOES SHOW UP AT THE POOL, offer them the Cool Off Party menu and a game of water volleyball. It's great exercise and guaranteed to be refreshing.

COOL OFF PARTY

Vegetable-Stuffed Mushrooms
Cool 'n' Spicy Gazpacho

❦ ❦ ❦

Poolside Marinated Chicken Breasts
Oven Fries

❦ ❦ ❦

Orange-Raspberry Delight
Sparkling Citrus Blend

❦ ❦ ❦

Vegetable-Stuffed Mushrooms

16 large mushrooms
¼ cup minced bell pepper
¼ cup minced onion
¼ cup chopped water
   chestnuts
¼ cup nonfat plain yogurt
½ teaspoon garlic powder
¼ teaspoon onion powder

Clean mushrooms. Remove mushrooms stems from caps; set caps aside. Finely chop stems, and mix with bell pepper, onion, and water chestnuts; set aside. Combine yogurt with garlic powder and onion powder; then add vegetable mixture. Steam mushroom caps just until tender; drain and then fill each with a heaping spoonful of vegetable mixture.

Yield: 16 filled mushrooms

Nutrients per mushroom:

Calories 12 Fat 0 g Carbohydrate 2 g Protein 1 g Sodium 2 g Cholesterol 0 mg

Cool 'n' Spicy Gazpacho

1 cup no-added-salt tomato
   juice
½ cup minced onion
3 tomatoes, chopped
1 clove garlic, minced
1 tablespoon olive oil
1 tablespoon lemon juice
¼ teaspoon cayenne pepper
¼ teaspoon hot sauce
1 large green pepper, finely
   chopped
1 cucumber, diced

Combine all ingredients. Mix well. Chill several hours before serving.

Yield: 6 servings

Nutrients per serving:

Calories 63 Fat 2 g Carbohydrate 8 g Protein 2 g Sodium 9 mg Cholesterol 0 mg

Poolside Marinated Chicken Breasts

1½ tablespoons lemon juice
4½ tablespoons cider vinegar
1½ tablespoons black pepper
1½ tablespoons honey
¾ teaspoon minced garlic
1½ pounds boneless, skinless
   chicken breasts

Combine lemon juice, vinegar, pepper, honey, and garlic. Pierce chicken breasts, and place in a shallow pan. Pour marinade over chicken, turning once to coat both sides. Refrigerate at least one hour.

Marinated chicken breasts can be grilled, baked, or broiled.

Yield: 6 servings

Nutrients per serving:

Calories 116 Fat 2 g Carbohydrate 0 g Protein 24 g Sodium 63 mg Cholesterol 72 mg

Oven Fries

6 medium-size white
   potatoes
Nonfat cooking spray
Black pepper

Preheat oven to 350°. Cut potatoes into thin wedges, about 4 to 6 per potato. Spray pan with cooking spray; arrange potato wedges on pan. Sprinkle with black pepper. Bake in oven 15 to 20 minutes or until crispy on the outside and fork tender inside, turning once during cooking time.

Yield: 6 servings

Nutrients per serving:

Calories 110 Fat 0 g Carbohydrate 23 g Protein 3 g Sodium 10 g Cholesterol 0 mg

Orange-Raspberry Delight

1 cup boiling water
1 (4-serving) package sugar-free raspberry gelatin
1 quart orange juice
1 (8-ounce) container light whipped topping

Combine water and gelatin mix in bowl. Stir in orange juice. Pour mixture into a freezer-safe container, and freeze until partially frozen. Remove from freezer. Stir to a smooth consistency; then gently fold in whipped topping. Return to freezer until fully frozen. Serve at room temperature.

Yield: 6 servings

Nutrients per serving:

Calories 155 Fat 5 g Carbohydrate 27 g Protein 2 g Sodium 85 mg Cholesterol 0 mg

Sparkling Citrus Blend

2 cups orange juice
1 cup grapefruit juice
½ cup ginger ale
2 tablespoons lemon juice
2 cups seltzer water

Combine all ingredients; mix well. Serve chilled.

Yield: 6 cups

Nutrients per 1 cup:

Calories 73 Fat 0 g Carbohydrate 17 g Protein 1 g Sodium 3 mg Cholesterol 0 mg

Eating well today means a lot less fat and a lot more vegetables, fruits, and foods make from grains like rice, pasta, and cereals.

Church Picnic

Breaking Bread

The word "companion" is derived from the Latin words *com* and *panis*, which combine to mean "one with whom you break bread." This, in the ancient world was a sign of true friendship and brotherhood—for one would never waste the staff of life on any lesser sort of character. And so it is today with the church picnic. It is a time for the congregation to come together to celebrate another year as an outward witness of Christ's body.

The picnic is an excuse to get together and be at one with one another. Everyone is on his best behavior. That is, until all the sugar from the brownies, cookies, and Koolaid hits the bloodstreams of the 5-year-olds. Decorum goes out the window as the games for the youngsters begin. A frenzied game of freeze-tag erupts into short-lived mayhem, resulting in a pants leg being ripped, grass stains galore, and potato salad being stomped on by a little boy in flight. But no one usually gets upset about these things on this day of fellowship.

Food is such an integral part of the church picnic. Once the thanks are given, the long line sets out past the folding tables, with everyone positioning themselves to reach the best dishes. The plates begin to creak and bow under the ever-increasing pressure of food as it piles up, as if to imitate the Tower of Babel. Many feats of engineering are accomplished as people in the congregation load their plates.

Meatloaf mingles with fried chicken, which mingles with a slab of lasagna, which sets upon green beans, baked beans, and three-bean salad. Mashed potatoes with gravy run into carrot and raisin salad, which is flanked by baked macaroni and cheese. And this is before one gets a smaller plate for the fruit salad, gelatin, cookies, lemon bars, and pie.

Once this is accomplished, folks settle down to some serious eating and fellowship with other members of the congregation. This is the time to actually sit and talk and get to know each other. The chat is usually edifying and good-hearted, not gossipy hearsay. Somehow the church picnic always seems to bring out a sincere goodness in people that is not often found in our busy world where people seldom have time to chat about nothing in general—just being friendly and breaking bread.

Kevin Bullard
Dallas, TX

ADMIT IT; everyone has always wanted to do this. Before the benediction, slip out to "use the restroom." With this tactic, you can scope out the various food lines to see which has homemade macaroni and cheese versus the boxed variety. Or which has the homemade chocolate cake rather than the store-bought one. Once you've decided on the line of choice, position yourself nearby. (Get your iced tea, and nonchalantly add the sugar and lemon so you look busy.) Then as people head to the tables, call a friend over to see how their week has been. This will throw even more suspicion away from your true motives.

HOLD THE CHURCH PICNIC AT A LOCATION OTHER THAN THE CHURCH GROUNDS. Choose a spot that offers lots of activities so everyone can stay busy. For instance, rent a miniature golf course that has picnic facilities. This provides the entertainment plus a place to set up the food. You can even have someone cater it and pay one price for the food and fun.

F EAST   OF   F UN

Pineapple Slaw
Pea and Cheese Salad

❦ ❦ ❦

Colorful Vegetable Chunks
Surf's Up Tuna

❦ ❦ ❦

Peachy Combo
Fruity Iced Tea

❦ ❦ ❦

Pineapple Slaw

2 pounds shredded cabbage
1 (8-ounce) can pineapple
  tidbits, drained
1 large apple, chopped
1 cup nonfat honey Dijon
  dressing

Toss cabbage with pineapple and apple. Pour dressing over cabbage-fruit mixture, and mix well. Chill thoroughly.

Yield: 6 servings

Nutrients per serving:

Calories 165 Fat 0 g Carbohydrate 40 g Protein 0 g Sodium 448 mg Cholesterol 0 g

Pea and Cheese Salad

1½ cups green peas
½ cup diced reduced-fat
  Cheddar cheese
½ cup diced onion
½ cup diced red bell pepper

Combine all ingredients; toss well. Serve chilled.

Yield: 6 servings

Nutrients per serving:

Calories 99 Fat 3 g Carbohydrate 8 g Protein 8 g Sodium 137 mg Cholesterol 13 mg

Including five fruits and vegetables daily can be easier than you might think; it just takes a little planning.

Colorful Vegetable Chunks

1 cup zucchini wedges
1 cup yellow squash wedges
1 cup chopped onion
1 cup red bell pepper
  chunks
Nonfat dressing

Combine all ingredients. Serve with choice of nonfat dressings.

Yield: 6 servings

Nutrients per serving:

Calories 32 Fat 0 g Carbohydrate 4 g Protein 1 g Sodium 1 g Cholesterol 0 mg

Surf's Up Tuna

3 (6½-ounce) cans water-
  packed tuna
6 tablespoons nonfat blue
  cheese dressing
1 tablespoon black pepper
6 tablespoons chopped
  onion
6 tablespoons chopped
  green bell pepper

Combine all ingredients. Chill well before serving.

Yield: 6 servings

Nutrients per serving:

Calories 127 Fat 1 g Carbohydrate 4 g Protein 25 g Sodium 421 mg Cholesterol 0 mg

Peachy Combo

4 medium nectarines
4 medium apricots
4 medium peaches
½ cup brown sugar
2 tablespoons cinnamon

Cut fruit into large chunks, and toss lightly. Mix brown sugar and cinnamon together; stir into fruit. Cover and refrigerate several hours. Serve chilled or at room temperature.

Yield: 8 servings

Nutrients per serving:

Calories 113 Fat 0 g Carbohydrate 29 g Protein 1 g Sodium 4 mg Cholesterol 0 mg

Fruity Iced Tea

4 tea bags
1 quart boiling water
1 quart cold water
1 cup orange juice
Orange rings (optional)

Place tea bags in a 1-gallon, heat-tempered pitcher, and fill with boiling water. Steep tea until cool. Remove tea bags, add cold water and juice; mix well. Chill and serve over ice. Garnish with orange rings, if desired.

Yield: 8 (1-cup) servings

Nutrients per cup:

Calories 20 Fat 0 g Carbohydrate 5 g Protein 0 g Sodium 0 mg Cholesterol 0 mg

Fourth of July

Holiday Magic

Lately, I find myself wondering whether holidays, as we spent them in child-hood, have vanished, or whether it is I who have simply grown up and past the wonder. When I was a child, I thought these special days "just happened." Although today I am well aware of the work that made them so special, I think that there was also an intangible element, an elixir of time and place and people, that imbued the holidays of my childhood with an innocence and joy that can be replaced but never duplicated, regardless how we try. The magic was unique to an age. And that age has passed for all of us. No holiday makes me believe this more than the Fourth of July.

My cousins, my brother, and I always spent the night of July 3rd at our grandparents' house, nestled in cool white sheets, giggling, telling jokes, and ultimately sleeping like rocks in preparation for the big day. We woke to the smell of buttermilk biscuits, breakfast pork chops, and grits laden with Cheddar cheese. Then there was the mailbox to decorate or the parade to prepare a float for or the lake to play in. The lake was a dense green color like an army tank and warm as bath water for the first 3 feet down, where our toes touched cold like the grasp of a witch's claw and we snatched them away from her reach. That's where we spent most of the day, reeking of algae and catfish bait, the necks of life preservers pressed against our chests.

And in between swimming, sailing, and catching bream, we ate Rotel dip and Fritos, peppered steak sandwiches, and chunks of watermelon we held in our hands, ignoring the juice that ran down our chins because as soon as we finished we jumped back in the lake. And all day long we smelled the ribs Grandfather cooked on a big brick grill, and our mouths watered. Because that was the finale—what we couldn't wait for.

Stunned by lake water, slightly sunburned, we raced through showers and into clean shorts. Barefoot, wet hair combed back, we found our seats on the porch facing the lake and filled our plates with ribs, potato salad, baked beans, and slaw. Ravenous from the sun and the water, we ate and ate, cicadas humming and mayflies, attracted by the light, landing on the screens. And as the fading sun turned the sky a deep purple, we poured chocolate sauce over homemade vanilla ice cream and waited for the fireworks, our fireworks, to begin.

Dawn Baldwin
Memphis, TN

THIS HOLIDAY IS A GREAT TIME to plan a trip to Philadelphia for a true look at our country's independence. The city usually observes the Fourth of July with a 3- or 4-day celebration. The Liberty Bell and Independence Hall are two must-sees. For more information, call the Philadelphia Visitors Center at (215) 636-1666. You also may want to lounge on the nearby beaches of Atlantic City, New Jersey.

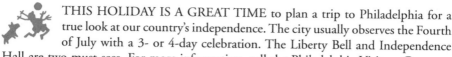 SPARKLERS ARE A MUST for everyone to try. Also light them, and place them on the top of the cake before you present it.

FIREWORKS DELIGHT

Mustard Spread
Creamy Potato Salad

🐸 🐸 🐸

Stuffed Hot Dogs
Fourth of July Salad

🐸 🐸 🐸

Independence Flag Cake
Raspberry Slurper

🐸 🐸 🐸

Mustard Spread

½ cup prepared mustard
1 teaspoon parsley
1 teaspoon horseradish
1 tablespoon dried onion
  flakes

Combine all ingredients. Mix well. Use as a spread on hot dogs, hamburgers, or sandwiches.

Yield: about ¾ cup

Nutrients per tablespoon:

Calories 10 Fat 0 g Carbohydrate 2 g Protein 0 g Sodium 150 mg Cholesterol 0 mg

Creamy Potato Salad

4 medium potatoes
½ cup nonfat sour cream
½ cup nonfat mayonnaise
½ cup chopped celery
½ cup chopped onion
1 teaspoon black pepper

Cook potatoes until soft; peel and dice them. Combine potatoes with remaining ingredients; mix well. Chill before serving.

Yield: 6 servings

Nutrients per serving:

Calories 180 Fat 0 g Carbohydrate 22 g Protein 4 g Sodium 32 mg Cholesterol 0 mg

Stuffed Hot Dogs

4 turkey hot dogs
2 tablespoons finely chopped green bell pepper
2 tablespoons finely chopped onion
4 hot dog buns

Partially split hot dogs. Mix bell pepper and onion together. Fill each hot dog with 1 tablespoon pepper-onion mixture. Grill over charcoal, split side up, in covered barbecue pit to cook thoroughly. Serve in hot dog buns.

Yield: 4 servings

Nutrients per serving:

Calories 221 Fat 10 g Carbohydrate 23 g Protein 9 g Sodium 695 mg Cholesterol 40 mg

Fourth of July Salad

3 medium tomatoes, sliced
3 cucumbers, sliced
1 onion, sliced
¾ cup white vinegar
1 tablespoon black pepper

Combine vegetables. Mix vinegar with pepper; pour over vegetables, and toss lightly. Chill before serving.

Yield: 8 servings

Nutrients per serving:

Calories 41 Fat 0 g Carbohydrate 7 g Protein 2 g Sodium 5 mg Cholesterol 0 mg

Celebrate your independence from high-fat foods!

Independence Flag Cake

2 angel food cake mixes
1 (8-ounce) container whipped topping
¾ cup blueberries
2 cups raspberries

Prepare cake according to package directions; bake in two 9 x 5-inch loaf pans. When loaves are cool, remove from pans, and arrange side by side. Frost with whipped topping. Decorate with fruit, placing blueberries close in upper left corner with even bits of white in between to create the white stars; line raspberries evenly over remaining cake for the red stripes. Serve immediately or keep chilled.

Yield: 12 servings

Nutrients per serving:

Calories 178 Fat 1 g Carbohydrate 39 g Protein 3 g Sodium 312 mg Cholesterol 0 mg

Raspberry Slurper

1 (6-ounce) package frozen raspberries
1 cup ginger ale
1 cup water
10 ice cubes

Combine all ingredients in blender; blend until smooth. Serve immediately.

Yield: 4 servings

Nutrients per serving:

Calories 81 Fat 0 g Carbohydrate 21 g Protein 0 g Sodium 5 mg Cholesterol 0 mg

County Fair

Carnies, Critters, and County Fairs

Ever wonder what a medieval marketplace festival in 1595 must have been like—grown men chasing farm animals, great booths of merchandise, and exciting contests of strength and skill? Just go to the county fair.

My childhood memories are rife with recollections of summer dog days, of my excitement when people from all the villages comprising the Sioux County Metroplex, and from all the farms in between, made fast of the county fair, held in my otherwise sleepy little town of Sioux Center, Iowa.

For me, the long buildings filled with prize-winning Holstein, Hereford, and Angus cattle, hogs, and other critters were serious entertainment. An afternoon could pass like nothing as marveled in the sight, feel, and—oh, boy—the aroma of these much cared-for animals. Neither will I forget the commercial buildings where, even as an adult, my goal was to snag as much free stuff as three days and my familiar face would allow.

Besides being a time of entertainment, the county fair was also an important part of my rural community's livelihood. The fair provided farmers with the opportunity to bid on livestock, to discuss the latest agriculture legislation, and to climb all over the tractor displays. Most people also enjoyed attending the infamous tractor pull contests; I never knew what was going on, but with the roar and the cheers and the smell of diesel in the air, I never missed it.

Then the night came. Ah, yes, the Iowa summer night. Warm breezes blew away the oppressive heat of the day, and out came the stars. Incidentally, the evening's midway carnival also enticed some of the more "interesting" people in my county to go a-fairin'. I was never sure where some of them hid out during the rest of the year, but something about the smell of popcorn; the dull, happy noise of chattering crowds; and the myriad lights illuminating the thrilled faces on carnival rides seemed to compel everyone to get along. This was a time of celebration! It mattered little if the "carnies" working the rides were a bit rough-cut, or if cotton candy prices were outrageous, or if you just couldn't get the little bulldozers to push any quarters into the money trough—this was the county fair, and you'd better enjoy it because it would soon be gone. Like a great medieval market day, the fair signaled a chance to combine work and play in what may be the greatest summer tradition ever. Except here, unlike 1595 England, you don't have to watch where you step—we keep the cows in pens!

Daniel Mennega
Sioux Center, IA

HEAD TO THE COUNTY FAIR EARLY, and get a good parking spot. Pack a big basket meal to avoid getting sick on cotton candy and greasy fried foods. And, most of all, *do not* climb into the bull pen.

 IF YOU'RE TRAVELING THROUGH IOWA AROUND JULY 4TH, head to the annual Sioux County Fair held in Sioux Center, about 45 miles north of Sioux City. For details, contact the Sioux County Extension Service at (712) 737-4230.

FAIR FARE

Shrimp Dip
Layered Veggies

🍎 🍎 🍎

Picnic Turkey Salad
Squash 'n' Pasta Salad

🍎 🍎 🍎

Light and Luscious Layers
Light 'n' Tangy Spritzer

🍎 🍎 🍎

Shrimp Dip

1 (8-ounce) package nonfat
   cream cheese
2 tablespoons skim milk
2 teaspoons lemon juice
1 (4½-ounce) can shrimp,
   rinsed and drained

*Combine cream cheese, milk, and
lemon juice. Mix with shrimp.
Serve with fresh vegetable dippers.*

Yield: about 2 cups

Nutrients per 1 tablespoon serving:

Calories 20 g Fat 0 g Carbohydrate 1 g Protein 4 g Sodium 33 mg Cholesterol 13 mg

Layered Veggies

1 quart shredded lettuce
1½ cups cucumber slices
1 cup red onion rings
1 (8-ounce) bottle nonfat
   red wine and vinegar
   dressing

*Combine first 3 ingredients; toss
with dressing. Chill until ready to
serve.*

Yield: 4 servings

Nutrients per serving:

Calories 132 g Fat 0 g Carbohydrate 25 g Protein 6 g Sodium 18 mg Cholesterol 0 mg

Picnic Turkey Salad

12 ounces cooked turkey
   breast, diced
1 cup bean sprouts
1 medium zucchini squash,
   sliced
¾ cup nonfat Italian
   dressing

Combine turkey and vegetables. Add dressing; toss to coat mixture.

Yield: 4 servings

Nutrients per serving:

Calories 175 g Fat 7 g Carbohydrate 3 g Protein 26 g Sodium 895 mg Cholesterol 59 mg

Squash 'n' Pasta Salad

4 cups cooked rainbow
   pasta twists
1 cup red wine vinegar
1 cup zucchini slices
1 cup yellow squash slices

Toss pasta lightly with red wine vinegar. Stir in squash slices.

Yield: 6 servings

Nutrients per serving:

Calories 145 g Fat 0 g Carbohydrate 31 g Protein 5 g Sodium 253 mg Cholesterol 0 mg

Pasta is a high-energy food—full of complex carbohydrates for regular fitness fans.

Light and Luscious Layers

1 package angel food cake
  mix
8 medium strawberries,
  halved
1 cup raspberries
¾ cup light whipped
  topping
Sprinkle of green colored
  sugar

Prepare cake mix per package directions, baking in two 9 x 5-inch loaf pans. After removing from pan, slice each loaf horizontally. Spread bottom layers with strawberries. Add top layer of cake, and top that layer with raspberries. Serve each slice with 1 tablespoon of light whipped topping and a sprinkle of sugar.

Yield: 12 servings

Nutrients per serving:

Calories 160 g Fat 0 g Carbohydrate 40 g Protein 0 g Sodium 0 mg Cholesterol 0 mg

Light 'n' Tangy Spritzer

1 quart diet lemon-lime
  soda
1 quart cranberry cocktail
2 cups orange juice

Mix soda, cranberry cocktail, and juice together. Refrigerate before serving.

Yield: approximately 13 (6-ounce) servings

Nutrients per serving:

Calories 80 g Fat 0 g Carbohydrate 20 mg Protein 0 g Sodium 0 mg Cholesterol 0 mg

Bridal Shower

Into Every Life a Little Shower Must Fall

If I had back all the money I've spent on other people's lingerie and kitchen appliances, I'd be a wealthy woman. In the last two years, everyone I know has decided to get married, giving me a steady stream of showers to attend. I've been to teas, suppers, dessert parties, Christmas showers, recipe showers, display showers, and pantry showers. Showers in sorority houses, grandmother's houses, and cramped college dorm rooms. If it involves wearing hose, bringing a gift, and drinking punch, I've done it—and usually with bad luck.

I'm the woman who gets "4 a.m." for 'round the clock showers, the "conservatory" for house showers, and the letter "Q" for alphabet showers. I've spilt red punch on antique tablecloths, and I always leave buying wrapping paper to the last minute, only to discover that Piggly Wiggly is out of everything but Garfield. That's why I was intrigued when I received an invitation to a "campsite shower" at a nearby state park for my friend Jill. No hose or priceless linens, and I could select a gift without alphabet or time restrictions.

Then I realized that Laura, a sorority sister, was having a lingerie shower the same day, a half-hour earlier. No problem, I could stay at Laura's long enough to make an appearance and drop off her gift, then head to the park. Pleased with my solution, I rushed to the mall to shop. I even had the department store wrap both gifts to prevent a last-minute trip to the Piggly Wiggly.

Sitting in the park the next day enjoying the weather, the company, and the brownies, I watched Jill unwrap pots and pans, a kerosene lantern, and fishing gear. I smiled as she opened my gift, pleased with the originality of my choice. She read the card out loud. "Best wishes for your adventures together. Love, Nancy." Jill didn't look delighted by my creativity, but a little surprised as she carefully unwrapped the tissue paper to reveal a lovely cream robe—the gift I had chosen for Laura. I was more than a little embarrassed and just sat there, speechless. Fortunately, Jill laughed and said that the robe was just the right weight to carry in her backpack.

I can only imagine what Laura said to her room full of guests as, in the midst of lingerie and sachets, she opened a first-aid kit, complete with bug spray, bandages, and emergency flare, with a card from me that read "Best wishes for many romantic nights."

Nancy Crosthwaite
Sherman, TX

MONTHS-OF-THE-YEAR SHOWERS are not as common as some of the others that are regulars, and it gives the gift buyers a broader subject to explore for their purchases.

HANDYMAN AND YARDWORK SHOWERS offer men the chance to be involved in this wedding process. Couples showers usually end up being the most fun; the campsite idea would be a perfect couples event if the bride and groom love the outdoors. Stock the bar is another couples idea.

BOUQUET OF GOODIES

Creamed Spice Dip
Mushroom Salad

❧ ❧ ❧

Lite-Bite Tuna
Crunchy Greens

❧ ❧ ❧

Dreamy Strawberry Pie
Lemon Tea Fizz

❧ ❧ ❧

Creamed Spice Dip

1 cup nonfat sour cream
1 cup nonfat yogurt
2 tablespoons onion
  powder
¼ cup minced onions

Blend sour cream and yogurt; stir in onion powder and onion. Chill. Serve as a dip with raw vegetables.

Yield: about 2½ cups

Nutrients per tablespoon:

Calories 7 Fat 0 g Carbohydrate 1 g Protein 1 g Sodium 8 mg Cholesterol 3 mg

Mushroom Salad

1 cup mushrooms
½ cup carrots
¼ cup onions
¼ cup red bell pepper
½ cup nonfat red wine
  vinegar dressing

Mix vegetables together. Add dressing; toss lightly.

Yield: 6 servings

Nutrients per serving:

Calories 19 Fat 0 g Carbohydrate 4 g Protein 0 g Sodium 257 mg Cholesterol 0 mg

Besides being naturally low in fat, fruits and vegetables eaten daily can be easier than you might think.

Lite-Bite Tuna Salad

2 (6½-ounce) cans water-packed tuna
4 tablespoons vinegar
2 teaspoons lemon juice
2 teaspoons lemon pepper seasoning
½ cup seasoned breadcrumbs

Combine all ingredients. Chill before serving.

Yield: 4 servings

Nutrients per serving:

Calories 160 Fat 2 g Carbohydrate 9 g Protein 26 g Sodium 395 mg Cholesterol 0 mg

Crunchy Greens

1 cup chopped romaine lettuce
1 cup chopped Bibb lettuce
1 cup chopped endive lettuce
1 cup sliced onion
½ cup sliced mushrooms
Nonfat dressing

Combine first 5 ingredients. Toss lightly. Serve with nonfat dressing.

Yield: 4 servings

Nutrients per serving:

Calories 40 Fat 0 g Carbohydrate 10 g Protein 0 g Sodium 40 mg Cholesterol 0 mg

Dreamy Strawberry Pie

1 (4-serving) package sugar-
  free strawberry-flavored
  gelatin mix
1 pint fresh strawberries,
  stemmed and quartered
1 cup light whipped
  topping
1 graham cracker crust

Prepare gelatin as directed on package; add fruit when slightly thickened; then gently fold in whipped topping. Pour into crust. Chill until firm.

Yield: 6 servings

Nutrients per serving:

Calories 164 Fat 7 g Carbohydrate 19 g Protein 2 g Sodium 220 mg Cholesterol 0 mg

Lemon Tea Fizz

4 tea bags
1 quart boiling water
1 quart cold water
2 cups diet lemon-lime soda
Lemon rings (optional)

Place tea bags in a 1-gallon, heat-tempered pitcher, and fill with boiling water. Steep tea until cool. Remove tea bags, add cold water and soda, mix well. Chill and serve over ice. Garnish with lemon rings, if desired.

Yield: 10 cups

Nutrients per 1 cup:

Calories 1 Fat 0 g Carbohydrate 10 g Protein 0 g Sodium 0 mg Cholesterol 0 mg

Day at the Lake

Relaxation in Georgia

The weatherman predicted a steamy June Saturday, so several friends, my roommate and I, and three dogs drove to Lake Hartwell in the northeast Georgia mountains. What better way to cool off than by the lake. The water was clear blue green and calm as we took off in the 19-foot Bayliner and headed toward the South Carolina waters. We found our favorite cove and proceeded to swim and sunbathe. The sun was bright and hot, so I was glad I had packed sunscreen and my purple-and-pink umbrella for protection. After a late lunch of grilled turkey sausage, baked beans, and baked potatoes, we decided to see if the fish were biting. While we were baiting our hooks, the dogs sat nearby and eyed us curiously. My roommate cast her line, and Whoopie, the black bulldog darted to the back of the boat and plopped into the deep water after the bait. Thank goodness she was wearing her yellow life vest. We pulled Whoopie back to the boat and found her exhausted but uninjured. She was rather cautious about the edge of the boat the rest of the day.

On the return trip to the marina, we stopped to explore one of the small islands along the way. Not too long after we arrived, several flocks of squealing geese flew close overhead and landed on the island. Their squealing continued and seemed to be directed toward us. We quickly realized we had stumbled onto a nesting site for the geese and made a fast exit to the Bayliner. On the trip home, we laughed about Whoopie and the close call with the geese—things I will remember for years to come. However, even if there were no crazy highlights to recall, the best part of the day at Lake Hartwell was relaxing and sharing good times with friends.

Cynthia Eitnier
Atlanta, GA

NECESSITIES AT THE LAKE: suntan lotion, a hat, clothes to cover with for less sun exposure, lots of liquids (preferably nonalcoholic), towels, book, music, and rubber floats.

 IF YOU'RE CATCHING FISH TO EAT, make sure you have a cooler filled with ice to keep them fresh.

ONLY KEEP THOSE YOU'LL USE. If a fish is too small or you have more than you need, use the catch-and-release method and send them back home. Barbless hooks are the most humane to fish with when practicing catch and release. If you can't find those, just take pliers and smash down the barb; this will accomplish the same effect.

LINGER AT LAKESIDE

Guacamole
Tangy Broccoli Cheese Spread

❦ ❦ ❦

Marinated Finger Slaw
Hawaiian Chicken Kebab

❦ ❦ ❦

Peachy Oatmeal Cookies
Tart 'n' Sweet Punch

❦ ❦ ❦

Guacamole

1 cup mashed avocado
¼ cup plain nonfat yogurt
¼ cup minced onion
1 tablespoon lime juice
1 clove garlic, minced
1 small jalapeño pepper, minced
⅛ teaspoon hot sauce

Blend avocado and yogurt together until smooth. Mix in remaining ingredients. Serve with oil-free tortilla chips.

Yield: about 2 cups

Nutrients per ¼ cup:

Calories 73 Fat 6 g Carbohydrate 5 g Protein 1 g Sodium 12 mg Cholesterol 0 mg

Tangy Broccoli Cheese Salad

3 cups chopped broccoli
1 medium Spanish onion, sliced
⅔ cup reduced-fat sharp Cheddar cheese
1 (8-ounce) bottle nonfat Italian dressing

Toss broccoli with onion. Stir in Cheddar cheese; add dressing, and stir lightly to coat all ingredients.

Yield: 6 servings

Nutrients per serving:

Calories 73 Fat 2 g Carbohydrate 9 g Protein 5 g Sodium 831 mg Cholesterol 7 mg

Keep food covered from insects, and remember to return perishables to the cooler chest as soon as possible. Don't let them sit out for more than 1 hour. If possible, serve plates directly from the cooler.

Marinated Finger Slaw

2 cucumbers
1 red bell pepper
1 yellow bell pepper
1 (8-ounce) bottle reduced-
  calorie red wine vinegar
  and oil dressing

Cut vegetables into 2-inch strips. Toss together, and cover with dressing. Mix lightly; marinate in refrigerator one hour or longer.

Yield: 4 servings

Nutrients per serving:

Calories 160 Fat 10 g Carbohydrate 11 g Protein 2 g Sodium 62 mg Cholesterol 0 mg

Hawaiian Chicken Kebab

½ cup balsamic vinegar
1 tablespoon olive oil
1 tablespoon lemon juice
1 tablespoon parsley
1 teaspoon black pepper
1 pound chicken breasts,
  cubed
1 cup pineapple chunks
9 mushrooms, cut into
  chunks
1 large red bell pepper, cut
  into chunks
1 medium onion, cut into
  chunks

Combine vinegar, olive oil, lemon juice, parsley, and black pepper. Pour over chicken in shallow dish, and marinate in refrigerator one hour or longer. In vegetable steamer, cook vegetables for 1 minute. On four individual skewers, alternate chicken, pineapple, and vegetables. Grill over hot charcoal, brushing with remaining marinade while cooking.

Yield: 4 servings

Nutrients per serving:

Calories 171 Fat 7 g Carbohydrate 10 g Protein 25 g Sodium 66 mg Cholesterol 72 mg

Peachy Oatmeal Cookies

1 cup peach-apple sauce
¾ cup brown sugar
¾ cup white sugar
1 teaspoon vanilla
2 eggs
1¼ cups flour
1 teaspoon baking soda
1 teaspoon cinnamon
3 cups quick-cooking oats

Preheat oven to 325°. Cream fruit sauce, sugars, vanilla, and eggs; set aside. Sift flour, baking soda, and cinnamon together. Stir into fruit sauce mixture; then stir in oats, and mix well.

Drop batter by tablespoonfuls onto greased cookie sheets. Bake 8 to 10 minutes.

Yield: 3 dozen cookies

Nutrients per cookie:

Calories 75 Fat 3 g Carbohydrate 16 g Protein 2 g Sodium 15 mg Cholesterol 12 mg

Tart 'n' Sweet Punch

3 cups orange juice
½ cup lemon juice
2 cups ginger ale
2 cups pineapple juice
1 cup water
Pineapple slices (optional)

Combine first 5 ingredients. Chill before serving. Garnish with pineapple slices, if desired.

Yield: 8½ cups

Nutrients per 1 cup:

Calories 89 Fat 0 g Carbohydrate 23 g Protein 0 g Sodium 6 mg Cholesterol 0 mg

Outdoor Concerts

And the Angel Said Unto Him, "It's Cheaper at Ike's"

It's something about the summer night air that makes outdoor concerts institutions in my memory. I can remember back to elementary school, picnicking to Beethoven on the lawn of the Dixon Art Gallery with my parents or listening to chamber music on the broken-down park benches at the Memphis Shell. As I grew up, the experiences moved from classical music to Jimmy Buffet or Eric Clapton. Or, as in the case of this story, Steppenwolf.

During one-of-many summertime roadtrips, some friends and I decided to splurge for a $3-a-ticket Steppenwolf concert on the banks of the Tennessee river in Chattanooga. The concert attendees included Tamara, Julie, Todd, and me—and the United Federation of Hell's Angels. Hell's Angels, for me, had always represented the rebellion and Harley in all of us, and the evening was quickly becoming a spiritual experience for me: Here I was, sitting on the riverbank with good friends, listening to an energetic (albeit so-so) band, and surrounded by a group of people who hovered at a level above the rest of us.

Of course, I experienced the common problems associated with events like this: We had to park 2 miles away, I was in the Job Johnny during the only Steppenwolf song I actually know (*Magic Carpet Ride*), someone tripped and spilt beer on my head—you know, the usual concert perks.

At one point in the evening, we walked past a small chorus of Angels in attendance: a woman with flaming red hair, leather pants, black boots, a leather vest, and a decoupage of roses across her chest; a man with multiple chains hanging from his leather pants; and a pit bull with a metal bone in its mouth.

What happened next was an experience I never expected, never wanted, and my world perceptions would be changed forever.

The man said, "Susie, I nicked my finger. Can we run by the Walgreen's before we head home?"

And Susie said, "No problem, honey, but maybe we should go by Ike's—I think it's a bit cheaper."

Irrevocably damaged. Crushed. Shattered. Without hope. My impression of Hell's Angels had, in the flash of a sentence, changed from a beer-guzzling, tattoo-laden, hairy-backed gang of bikers to normal people, to Bunyan's Everyman. As I have never recovered from this incident and continue to experience traumatic flashbacks of the overheard conversation, I now try to mind my own business at outdoor concerts, focusing instead on the music, the companionship, and the warm, starry-night sky.

Martha Hopkins
Memphis, TN

WHEN ATTENDING AN OUTDOOR SYMPHONY, show some class. Take along a colorful quilt, small plastic table, a cotton tablecloth, a small vase of flowers, and candles with holders. Fill the basket with items that are easy to pack and easy to eat. Use a small dolly cart to ease the transporting of your feast to that perfect spot.

ROCK CONCERTS DESERVE A MORE CASUAL APPROACH. A nice heavy blanket, a small basket of snacks, insect repellent, and possibly earplugs, in case you sit near the giant speakers.

WIPES FOR YOUR HANDS ARE HELPFUL when eating outside. You can buy them or make your own: Use heavy paper towels. Dip each towel in a mixture of sudsy water mixed with alcohol. Fold the towel, and place in zip-top bag. Make as many as needed.

CONCERT MEDLEY

Salsa
Crunchy Spinach and Mushroom Salad

🍎 🍎 🍎

Creamy Turkey Salad
Cucumber Salad

🍎 🍎 🍎

Sunrise Finale
Sparkling Punch

🍎 🍎 🍎

Salsa

1 cup chopped onion
1 tablespoon red wine
  vinegar
1 tablespoon oregano
1 tablespoon cumin powder
3 medium tomatoes,
  chopped
1 hot green chile pepper

Combine all ingredients. Mix well. Chill thoroughly. Serve with oil-free tortilla chips.

Yield: about 3 cups

Nutrients per ¼ cup:

Calories 13 Fat 0 g Carbohydrate 3 g Protein 0 g Sodium 3 mg Cholesterol 0 mg

Crunchy Spinach and Mushroom Salad

½ pound fresh spinach, torn
  into bite-size pieces
2 cups mushroom slices
1 cup diced red pepper
1 (14-ounce) can bean
  sprouts, drained
Fat-free dressing or soy
  sauce

Combine vegetables; toss to mix. Serve with choice of dressing or soy sauce.

Yield: 6 servings

Nutrients per serving:

Calories 47 Fat 0 g Carbohydrate 8 g Protein 3 g Sodium 64 mg Cholesterol 0 mg

Creamy Turkey Salad

1½ pounds cooked, skinned turkey breast, diced
1½ cups nonfat mayonnaise
1½ cups chopped celery
1 cup chopped onion
2 tablespoons salt-free lemon pepper seasoning
1½ cups chopped red bell pepper

Combine all ingredients. Chill before serving.

Yield: 8 servings

Nutrients per serving:

Calories 186 Fat 3 g Carbohydrate 13 g Protein 25 g Sodium 646 mg Cholesterol 59 mg

Cucumber Salad

3 medium cucumbers, sliced
1 large Spanish onion, chopped
1 tablespoon crushed basil
1 cup balsamic vinegar

Mix cucumbers and onion together; sprinkle with basil. Pour vinegar over vegetable mixture, and toss to coat. Chill before serving.

Yield: 6 servings

Nutrients per serving:

Calories 42 Fat 0 g Carbohydrate 7 g Protein 4 g Sodium 2 g Cholesterol 0 mg

Sunrise Finale

2 large oranges
2 large bananas
1 cup cherries, pitted
1 cup orange juice

Coarsely chop fruits; combine in a large bowl. Stir in orange juice. Serve chilled.

Yield: 6 servings

Nutrients per serving:

Calories 90 Fat 0 g Carbohydrate 21 g Protein 1 g Sodium 0 mg Cholesterol 0 mg

Sparkling Punch

1 quart orange juice
1 cup lemon juice
1 quart seltzer water
1 quart ginger ale

Combine all ingredients; mix well. Serve chilled.

Yield: 13 cups

Nutrients per 1 cup:

Calories 62 Fat 0 g Carbohydrate 15 g Protein 0 g Sodium 6 mg Cholesterol 0 mg

Take-along food for warm-weather activities needs to be properly stored. Use containers with good seals, baskets to keep out insects, and coolers for perishables.

Sweet Sixteen

The Best Laid Plans

A giggly pool party. Heart-shaped cake with thick icing. My very own set of keys to the family car....Wait, make that a shiny new convertible in the driveway, sporting a gigantic red bow. Much better.

Ahh, the dreams of a soon-to-be sweet-sixteener.

It's funny how our expectations don't *quite* match up with what really happens. Sometimes they're not even close. My actual recollections of that milestone birthday include me and a six-pack of calamine lotion, frequent oatmeal baths, and strict orders not to scratch. After sixteen years and many chances at exposure, I dodged the proverbial chicken pox bullet no longer.

Believe me when I say that I was *not* one of those people who lucked out with a "light case," showing off their three pox. Not me. One of my days in quarantine I decided to count and gave up somewhere after 300.

Now, I know no one's driver's license picture is perfect, mind you, but, looking in the mirror, there was NO WAY I was going to venture down to the DMV for several weeks, license or no license.

I think the most ironic part of my sixteenth birthday was that on the day that I was to feel the most grown-up, I was sitting on a Mickey Mouse-sheet-covered couch, itching, stuck at home with a little kids' disease. Scratch, scratch.

But it wasn't really so bad. I had a second Spring Break. My mom catered my pox party with all my favorite foods and a carton of mint chocolate chip ice cream. That week we rented movies—lots of movies—seventeen to be exact (one to grow on, you know). And I got those family car keys: on a shiny new key chain, with a bright red bow. I was feeling much better.

Jenny Bech
St. Charles, IL

RENT *Sixteen Candles* as one of those must-see videos for that special day.

 EVERY 16-YEAR-OLD FEMALE WOULD LOVE to have a makeover package for her birthday—new hairdo, manicure, maybe even a facial.

HAVE THE CREST OF THE FAMILY NAME MADE into a ring or pendant, and as each child in the family turns 16, present them with the ring or pendant.

16-CANDLE SALUTE

Stuffed Mushroom Caps
Simple Spinach Salad

Grilled Ham Steak
Pasta Twists

Fruit 'n' Cream Crush
Strawberry Lemonade

❦ ❦ ❦

Stuffed Mushroom Caps

16 large mushrooms
¼ cup minced celery
¼ cup minced onion
¼ cup nonfat mayonnaise
½ teaspoon garlic powder
¼ cup breadcrumbs

Remove mushroom stems from caps; set caps aside. Finely chop stems, and mix with remaining ingredients. Fill each mushroom cap with a spoonful of the mixture. Heat in vegetable steamer until warm. Serve immediately.

Yield: 16 appetizers

Nutrients per 1 mushroom:

Calories 16 Fat 0 g Carbohydrate 3 g Protein 1 g Sodium 60 mg Cholesterol 0 mg

Simple Spinach Salad

1 pound spinach, washed and torn
1 hard-cooked egg, chopped
4 slices turkey bacon, cooked and crumbled
1 tomato, cut into wedges
4 rice cakes, crumbled into chunks
1 teaspoon black pepper
Nonfat Italian dressing (optional)

Toss all ingredients together. Serve with dressing, if desired.

Yield: 6 servings

Nutrients per serving:

Calories 87 Fat 3 g Carbohydrate 10 g Protein 6 g Sodium 213 mg Cholesterol 43 mg

Grilled Ham Steak

½ cup pineapple juice
1 tablespoon honey
1 tablespoon brown sugar
12 ounces low-sodium, lean ham steak

Mix juice, honey, and brown sugar together. Grill ham over hot charcoals, basting frequently with juice mixture.

Yield: 4 servings

Nutrients per serving:

Calories 171 Fat 5 g Carbohydrate 9 g Protein 21 g Sodium 1128 mg Cholesterol 47 mg

Pasta Twists

2 cups cooked spiral pasta
½ cup chopped green bell pepper
½ cup chopped red bell pepper
4 strips turkey bacon, crumbled
1 cup nonfat red wine vinegar dressing

Combine pasta, bell peppers, and bacon. Stir in dressing, and toss well to coat all ingredients. Chill before serving.

Yield: 8 servings

Nutrients per serving:

Calories 80 Fat 1 g Carbohydrate 13 g Protein 3 g Sodium 480 mg Cholesterol 5 mg

Fruit 'n' Cream Crush

1½ cups (approximately 18)
    crushed vanilla wafers
1½ cups nonfat frozen vanilla
    yogurt, partially thawed
6 medium peaches, sliced
Nonfat whipped topping

Mix cookies and yogurt together. Spread into 13 x 9 x 2-inch rectangular pan. Freeze. Let stand at room temperature for 30 minutes; top with peaches and whipped topping. Serve immediately.

Yield: 8 to 10 servings

Nutrients per serving:

Calories 36 Fat 0 g Carbohydrate 8 g Protein 0 g Sodium 18 mg Cholesterol 2 mg

Strawberry Lemonade

¾ cup lemon juice
1 quart water
Powdered sugar substitute
    (equal to ½ cup powdered
    sugar)
½ cup pureed strawberries

Combine all ingredients in blender; mix at high speed until thoroughly blended. Serve well chilled.

Yield: 5 (1-cup) servings

Nutrients per serving:

Calories 14 Fat 0 g Carbohydrate 4 g Protein 0 g Sodium 0 mg Cholesterol 0 mg

Teen years are usually active ones and include a final "growth spurt" from Mother Nature. Most teens need not rely entirely on nonfat foods.

Block Party

A Neighborly Afternoon

Watermelon.

When I think of our block party in Rock Hill, Missouri, the first thing I remember is that oblong of green resting on a white tablecloth. Throughout that sunny afternoon in August 1990, neighborhood children sidled up to the watermelon table, their eyes shining and wide with expectation.

They had to wait for the melon, though. First things first: fried chicken, barbecued ribs, hot dogs, mustardy slaw, congealed fruit salad with cherries, baked beans, iced tea, beer, and a host of other goodies. Each dish had an "honest" taste—the pride of the maker was manifest in the careful seasoning, the just-right doneness of the meat.

As we returned to the buffet tables again and again, all the neighbors mingled, chatted, and got to know each other a little better. We had gathered just to celebrate being neighbors, the not uncommon forces of food and music drawing people together.

My husband, Carter, and I resided in an ethnically mixed neighborhood. We were black, Caucasian, and Asian. We were young, elderly, and middle-aged. No one was poor, no one was rich, but everybody was working hard to make ends meet. My husband described it as "barebones middle America."

After we ate, we danced on a black asphalt driveway to music provided by a disc jockey. There was group dancing, all of us trying to learn a series of complicated steps and laughing as we made mistakes. When the jockey played rap music by M. C. Hammer, the youngsters showed what they could do. When the doo-wop of the Four Tops came lilting over the speakers, their parents took the floor. Each group cheered the other along. As Carter put it, "There was something dichotomous but unifying about that asphalt dance floor."

Balloons and ice cream from a real ice-cream cart, conversation and laughter, shared music and good food. Those common elements combined to make us a neighborhood in the old-fashioned sense of the word. Those things and a watermelon.

As our neighbor, who was also our postman, raised a sharp, shiny knife, I watched the faces of the children gathered around the table. In these days of electronic games and fast food, something as simple and humble as a watermelon can still inspire the sweet, juicy goodness inside, everyone cheered again. For that moment, for that afternoon, we were one, our tenderness toward our fellow man exposed.

Virginia McAfee Davis
Memphis, TN

A THEME FOR AN ANNUAL BLOCK PARTY gives the neighbors a chance to explore their creativity. Try a shish-kebab party: Everyone brings cut up items to add to the skewers, and then folks can mix and match the ingredients. Lots of grills are needed for this type gathering as they would be for a fish fry. An appetizer party requires no cooking at the scene, so the neighbors can spend time visiting.

DON'T FORGET TO PLAN ACTIVITIES FOR THE KIDS. Make sure there's a big field where they can play kickball or softball, but also have some prepared games: 3-legged races, sack races, team relays. (Adults love these games as well.)

A BLOCK BUSTER

Grilled Vegetables
Greens, "Shroom," and Bacon Salad

❦ ❦ ❦

Barbecue Beef Sandwiches
Spicy Eggplant

❦ ❦ ❦

Crispy Blueberry Surprise
Tropical Cooler

❦ ❦ ❦

Grilled Vegetables

2 medium-size red potatoes,
  scrubbed
1 cup fresh baby carrots
2 medium zucchini
¼ cup olive oil

Cut potatoes into quarters. Steam carrots and potatoes in micro-wave or stove top vegetable steamer about 5 minutes. Cut zucchini into 2-inch sticks. Lightly brush all vegetables with olive oil. Grill directly on rack over medium hot coals (lay vegetables opposite to the grill openings so they do not fall through). Turn once, and con-tinue grilling until desired tenderness.

Yield: 6 servings

Nutrients per serving:

Calories 140 Fat 9 g Carbohydrate 12 g Protein 2 g Sodium 12 g Cholesterol 0 mg

Greens, "Shroom," and Bacon Salad

½ pound fresh spinach, torn
  into bite-size pieces
2 cups mushroom slices
1 cup diced red pepper
6 slices turkey bacon,
  cooked and crumbled
½ cup nonfat Italian
  dressing

Combine vegetables; toss to mix. Stir in turkey bacon. Sprinkle with dressing before serving.

Yield: 6 servings

Nutrients per serving:

Calories 80 Fat 3 g Carbohydrate 9 g Protein 26 g Sodium 437 mg Cholesterol 0 mg

Barbecue Beef Sandwiches

1½ pounds shredded round
   steak
1 large onion, sliced
1½ cups barbecue sauce
6 kaiser rolls

In nonstick pan, brown steak over medium heat. Add onion and barbecue sauce; simmer until thoroughly heated. For each sandwich, fill one roll with one-sixth of steak and sauce mixture; wrap sandwiches in aluminum foil to take to the party. Serve warm.

Yield: 6 servings

Nutrients per serving:

Calories 363 Fat 6 g Carbohydrate 42 g Protein 32 g Sodium 880 mg Cholesterol 71 mg

Spicy Eggplant

2 large eggplant
2 cups hot-and-spicy
   vegetable juice
½ cup vinegar
2 cups salsa

Slice eggplant into ½-inch rounds; place in shallow pan. Mix juice and vinegar together; pour over eggplant slices, and let marinate one hour or longer. Steam marinated eggplant in a microwave or stove top steamer until tender. Top each slice with 2 tablespoons salsa before serving. (Carry eggplant in foil-lined pan to keep warm.)

Yield: 8 servings

Nutrients per serving:

Calories 38 Fat 0 g Carbohydrate 10 g Protein 0 g Sodium 898 mg Cholesterol 0 mg

Crispy Blueberry Surprise

3 cups blueberries
½ cup light brown sugar
⅔ cup rolled oats
1 teaspoon cinnamon

Preheat oven to 375°. Spread blueberries in a nonstick 8-inch square pan. Mix brown sugar, oats, and cinnamon; sprinkle mixture over berries. Heat in oven until oats are slightly toasted. Serve warm or at room temperature.

Yield: 6 servings

Nutrients per serving:

Calories 40 Fat 0 g Carbohydrate 33 g Protein 1 g Sodium 0 mg Cholesterol 0 mg

Tropical Cooler

1 (12-ounce) can frozen pineapple juice concentrate
¼ cup lemon juice
1 (12-ounce) can frozen orange juice concentrate
2 quarts seltzer water

Combine all ingredients; mix well. Serve chilled.

Yield: about 12 cups

Nutrients per 1 cup:

Calories 100 Fat 0 g Carbohydrate 25 g Protein 0 g Sodium 0 mg Cholesterol 0 mg

Fat does carry flavor, so when eating with less fat, season well with your favorite herbs and spices.

Beach Blast

BIG RED: The Life Saver

Trips to the beach on St. Simon's Island always started in my grandmother's kitchen. After my sisters and I had packed the incidentals (towels and trowels, prickly straw mats, books, nets, and suntan lotion), Grandma assembled the real beach survival kit—the cooler.

She was commander in charge of our gastral gear. She would tally up our drink orders and dispatch one of us to fetch the bottles from the cool, dank storage shed out back. That shed must have been the only naturally cool place on the island in the summer, and it definitely was one of the creepiest. Grandpa kept all his garden tools there, as well as the squirrel tails and raccoon skins he used for his handmade fishing lures. Stepping from the bright haze of a Georgia sun into that tiny space meant momentary blindness until, like a blessing dangling from God above, you leapt up and yanked the light string on.

Once the ice and drinks were loaded into the smaller blue cooler, Grandma went to work on BIG RED. Fully stocked, that chest was stout enough to crush any one of us girls flat. She fixed crunchy peanut butter and grape jelly sandwiches. She tucked in fresh blueberry muffins, polka-dotted with the blue bounty of yesterday's adventure. She stacked tins of Beanie Weenies and trays of processed cheese spread and crackers. She tossed oranges and prunes in for good measure. And she sidetracked the snack threat with a cylinder of Pringles and a pillowed pile of Twinkies.

In those pre-fat-fearing days, Grandma was thankfully of the school that believed ice cream was good for growing kids because it was a dairy product. So she taped a few quarters to the inner sides of the chest for ice-cream stand visits. Nearly 20 pounds heavier than when she first assaulted it, BIG RED was good to go.

How we ever made it to the water, or even could pull ourselves away from our sand-spit concession stand long enough to dig a castle moat is beyond me. How we ate through the entire contents of the cooler without getting sick or growing into beached whales ourselves is also something of a mystery. But to this day, Grandma's beach starvation wisdom still proves true: There is something about the sand and the sun and swimming in saltwater that just makes a body hungry.

Melissa Bigner
Durham, NC

187

TO EXPLORE THE BEACHES OF ST. SIMONS ISLAND yourself, obtain more information by writing St. Simons Chamber of Commerce, 530-B Beachview Dr., St. Simons Island, GA. 31522; or call 1-800-525-8678.

 A PERFECT ENDING TO A DAY AT THE BEACH IS A CAMPFIRE (if it is legal). Roast marshmallows, and sing along with a guitar or banjo. Remember to pack a sweater or jacket; no matter how hot the day, an evening by the water is bound to be chilly.

BESIDES THE USUAL SUNTAN LOTION AND TOWELS, take a beach umbrella for some shade, and pack everything in plastic zip-top bags to keep out the sand.

B E A C H   B U F F E T

Chunky Bean Dip
Sea Shell Pasta

🦀 🦀 🦀

Shrimp Salad
Zesty Asparagus Spears

🦀 🦀 🦀

Berry Bikini Dessert
Thirst Quencher Limeade

🦀 🦀 🦀

Chunky Bean Dip

½ teaspoon cumin
1 cup salsa
¾ cup chopped green bell
    pepper
1 cup cooked black beans,
    coarsely chopped

Mix cumin with salsa. Add bell pepper and black beans. Serve with oil-free tortilla chips.

Yield: 2½ cups

Nutrients per (1 tablespoon) serving:

Calories 7 g Fat 0 g Carbohydrate 2 g Protein 0 g Sodium 61 mg Cholesterol 0 mg

Sea Shell Pasta

2 cups cooked shell pasta
1 cup cooked corn
¼ cup scallions
¼ cup chopped red bell
    pepper
¾ cup nonfat ranch dressing
1 teaspoon black pepper

Combine pasta and vegetables. Add dressing and pepper; mix well. Chill before serving.

Yield: 6 servings

Nutrients per serving:

Calories 122 Fat 0 g Carbohydrate 25 g Protein 3 g Sodium 300 mg Cholesterol 0 mg

Shrimp Salad

1½ pounds shrimp, peeled,
   deveined, and chopped
¾ cup chopped celery
¾ cup chopped onion
1½ cups nonfat mayonnaise
1½ teaspoons black pepper

*Combine all ingredients. Chill
before serving.*

Yield: 6 servings

Nutrients per serving:

Calories 155 Fat 1 g Carbohydrate 14 g Protein 21 g Sodium 997 mg Cholesterol 195
mg

Zesty Asparagus Spears

1½ cups bottled nonfat red
   wine and vinegar dressing
½ cup lemon juice
½ chopped parsley
24 medium spears asparagus

*Combine dressing with juice and
parsley. Cut asparagus spears in
half lengthwise. Pour dressing
mixture over spears, and marinate several hours before serving.*

Yield: 6 servings

Nutrients per serving:

Calories 49 Fat 0 g Carbohydrate 9 g Protein 1 g Sodium 802 mg Cholesterol 0 mg

Berry Bikini Dessert

1 cup strawberry halves
1 cup raspberries
1 cup blueberries
1 cup blackberries
Powdered sugar to taste

Gently mix fruit together. Spoon into six dessert dishes. Dust with powdered sugar.

Yield: 6 servings

Nutrients per serving:

Calories 43 Fat 0 g Carbohydrate 11 g Protein 0 g Sodium 2 mg Cholesterol 0 mg

Thirst Quencher Limeade

½ cup lime juice
1 quart water
2 cups diet lemon-lime
   flavored soda
¼ cup sugar
Lime slices (optional)

Combine all ingredients. Mix well. Serve chilled. Garnish with lime slices, if desired.

Yield: 6 (1-cup) servings

Nutrients per serving:

Calories 37 Fat 0 g Carbohydrate 9 g Protein 0 g Sodium 0 mg Cholesterol 0 mg

When enjoying active fun in the sun, drink plenty of fluids and include high-energy snacks.

Hiking

The Gender Difference

Spending a day trekking through nature is an event everyone should experience. The surrounding sights and sounds are awe-inspiring. But when jaunting into the woods, the two sexes may take opposing views of trail necessities.

Her Hiking Essentials:

- A good map—drawn to scale, of course—that shows elevations and the exact course of the trail. Possession of the map puts you in charge, in control—where a woman belongs.
- A watch with a sweep hand. For checking heart rate and maintaining optimum aerobic intensity, and also for monitoring rate of travel.
- Low-fat granola bars and fresh fruit to nourish your body. An occasional piece of hard candy will satiate the sweet tooth with minimal calories.
- Sturdy hiking boots. (They all make your feet look big—get over it.)
- A rugged flannel shirt. Bright reds, greens, and blues for cool palettes; earthy browns, yellows, and oranges for warm palettes.
- A bandana—in a complementary color—rolled and tied around the head. Essential for keeping perspiration out of the eyes.
- Conservative earrings to complete your ensemble—even in the woods where, yes, it's likely no one else will see you.
- Lipstick. Lips get chapped, and if you're going to moisten them, a little splash of color won't hurt.

His Hiking Essentials:

- Junk food. Why else would you be exercising if it wasn't to treat yourself.
- A solid pair of hiking boots. They're better for your feet than tennis shoes. Be sure they are an earthtone; no fluorescents or pastels.
- Cute puppy, if they're allowed. It guarantees women will talk to you.
- Shorts. No matter how warm or cold it is. It shows that you're not afraid of the elements, and makes your calves look good going up hills.
- No maps. You always know exactly where you are.
- No watch. Free spirits don't need them.
- A pocket knife. You can cut small limbs, string, and human flesh; you can also cut your fingernails and pick your teeth—very versatile.
- A bandana. You can wear it. If you have a sneezing fit, it can rescue you from the drips; if someone gets cut, it becomes a bandage.
- A cooler full of you favorite ice cold beverage. The image of a cold brewski at the end of the trail can be just the push you need.

Tracy and Tim Jackson
Birmingham, AL

THE GREAT SMOKY MOUNTAINS NATIONAL PARK, in Tennessee and North Carolina, is one of the most visited areas in the U.S. But many folks make the mistake of never leaving their cars. The park has more than 800 miles of trails, including the Appalachian Trail. Hiking maps can be obtained at all the visitors centers throughout the park.

 YOSEMITE NATIONAL PARK in central California and Mount Rainier National Park in Washington are worth exploring on the West coast.

GOOD HIKING SHOES, plenty of liquids, and bad-weather gear are musts for all serious hikers.

STATE PARKS IN YOUR REGION offer many hiking opportunities. Check with the headquarters located nearest to you.

PICNIC ON THE TRAIL

Corny Mallow Raisin Mix
Chunks o' Tomato

🐸 🐸 🐸

Backpackers' Vegetable Hoagie
Color-of-Summer Salad

🐸 🐸 🐸

Berry Chocolate Sugar Cookies
Grape-Sweetened Ice Water

🐸 🐸 🐸

Corny Mallow Raisin Mix

6 cups popped popcorn
3 cups raisins
2 cups miniature
   marshmallows

Combine all ingredients. Store in airtight containers or sealed bags.

Yield: about 10 cups

Nutrients per cup:

Calories 193 Fat 0 g Carbohydrate 50 g Protein 0 g Sodium 20 mg Cholesterol 0 mg

Chunks o' Tomato

3 medium tomatoes, diced
1 cup salsa
1 small green bell pepper,
   minced
1 cup tomato juice
½ cup vinegar

Mix tomatoes, salsa, and green pepper together. Combine juice and vinegar; pour over vegetable mixture, and mix well.

Yield: 6 servings

Nutrients per serving:

Calories 41 Fat 0 g Carbohydrate 9 g Protein 1 g Sodium 525 mg Cholesterol 0 mg

Outdoor activities, such as hiking, often require a little heartier fare.

Backpackers' Vegetable Hoagie

½ teaspoon olive oil
¼ cup zucchini squash
¼ cup yellow squash
¼ cup onion slices
¼ cup mushroom slices
1 (5-inch) submarine roll
2 slices nonfat American
  cheese
¼ teaspoon black pepper

*In a nonstick pan, heat olive oil,
and sauté vegetables. Line roll
with cheese slices; fill with vegetables. Sprinkle with black
pepper.*

Yield: 1 serving

Nutrients per hoagie:

Calories 352 Fat 7 g Carbohydrate 50 g Protein 21 g Sodium 1182 mg Cholesterol 0 mg

Color-of-Summer Salad

2 cups cooked corn
½ cup chopped red onion
1 large red bell pepper
1 cup nonfat Italian
  dressing

*Combine vegetables. Add dress-
ing; mix well to coat all ingredients.*

Yield: 6 servings

Nutrients per serving:

Calories 66 Fat 0 g Carbohydrate 16 g Protein 2 g Sodium 389 mg Cholesterol 0 mg

Berry Chocolate Sugar Cookies

¼ cup margarine
⅓ cup strawberry-apple sauce
⅔ cup sugar
1 large egg
¾ teaspoon vanilla extract
2 tablespoons skim milk
⅓ cup unsweetened cocoa powder
1½ cups flour
¼ teaspoon baking powder

Preheat oven to 350°. Combine margarine, fruit sauce, and sugar. Add egg, vanilla, milk, and cocoa; set aside. Combine flour and baking powder, and add to fruit sauce/cocoa mixture; mix well. Roll dough into table-spoon-size balls, and place on greased baking sheet approximately 1-inch apart. Flatten slightly. Bake about 8 minutes.

Yield: 3 to 4 dozen cookies

Nutrients per cookie:

Calories 32 Fat 1 g Carbohydrate 5 g Protein 1 g Sodium 12 mg Cholesterol 5 mg

Grape-Sweetened Ice Water

2 envelopes plain gelatin
1 cup water
1 (6-ounce) can frozen grape juice

Soften gelatin in 1 cup water in a small saucepan (about 5 minutes); dissolve gelatin over low heat, stirring constantly. Remove from heat; add grape juice concentrate, and mix well. Lightly coat ice cube trays with nonstick spray. Pour mixture into trays. Cover and freeze.
Add 10 frozen cubes to each quart of cold water.

Nutrients per 1 cup:

Calories 50 Fat 0 g Carbohydrate 12 g Protein 0 g Sodium 0 mg Cholesterol 0 mg

Back to School

The Circle Beckons

. . . .

Summers at my mother's house were spent, quite literally, out on the street. She lived on a cul-de-sac surrounded with ranch-style houses, fenced-in backyards, barking dogs, and anxious elementary school kids. These were my playmates, my pals, my partners in mischief, members of a tight-knit posse that used the street as our gathering place.

"The circle" was something of a circus ring. It was the meeting place for swimming pool pickups, a kickball court, even a giant chalkboard. Many days it was a baseball diamond, the manhole cover acting as the pitcher's mound. Other days, the circle was transformed into a race track, our bicycles serving as champion two-wheeled Thoroughbreds competing for the Triple Crown. My mother's steep driveway gave me a speedy entry into the ring, allowing my green banana-seat stallion a short-lived neck ahead of the pack.

By late August, the action moved out of the circle and down to the bus stop. The first few days of school were a mixed bag, beginning with everyone's parents standing with us for the bus. It was wearing stiff, itchy back-to-school outfits, comparing new book bags and lunch boxes. Back to school was the sound of the spine of new books cracking after being opened for the first time, the smell of pencil shavings, and the shrill shout of the school bell at 8 a.m. It was swapping sandwiches, scratch-n-sniff stickers, and show and tell.

For the first few weeks, the circle silently beckoned. It was all we could do to sit in our seats when the bus rounded the corner. New book bags flew just like the old ones, onto pavements scattered with new cardigan sweaters and jean jackets. The games would begin again, but they would be cut short by dinner bells and calls inside to do homework. But by the time the leaves began to change, the circle was something we looked at through windows.

It seems my back-to-school ritual has peaked. The circle is now a place where I park my car when I visit. And college has become the circus that the circle was, still connected in some way—only farther down the street. And I still come home to the circle, just not as often. It's funny how things work out like that.

Andrea Bigner
Greenville, SC

A PARENT-CHILD SHOPPING TRIP before school starts gets things off on the right track and serves as a time of bonding.

 Going back to school should be a special occasion, whether it's elementary, high school, or heading off to college. PLAN A SPECIAL PICNIC WITH YOUR CHILD, either as a family affair or with friends. Balloons and streamers are a must to make it festive. A small piñata filled with school supplies (and hard candies) provides the entertainment.

 AN END-OF-SUMMER HAYRIDE provides friends with a chance for the one big hurrah before getting down to business. End the hayride with a great fiesta picnic.

LATE-SUMMER FIESTA

Party Nachos
Taco Salad

❧ ❧ ❧

Light 'n' Spicy Beef Strips
Beans and Rice

❧ ❧ ❧

Peachy Surprise
Tart 'n' Tangy Punch

❧ ❧ ❧

Party Nachos

2 (6-inch) corn tortillas
1 cup tomato sauce
1 clove garlic, minced
¼ teaspoon cumin powder
¼ teaspoon chili powder
2 tablespoons sliced
    jalapeño peppers
4 ounces nonfat shredded
    mozzarella cheese

Preheat oven to 400°. Cut tortillas into wedges, and broil until crisp. Cover bottom of baking dish or cookie sheet with tortilla wedges. Mix tomato sauce with garlic, cumin, and chili powder; pour over tortillas. Top with jalapeños and cheese. Bake in oven 5 to 10 minutes or until cheese is melted and nachos are thoroughly warmed.

Yield: approximately 12 nachos

Nutrients per 3 nachos:

Calories 91 Fat 0 g Carbohydrate 12 g Protein 10 g Sodium 611 mg Cholesterol 5 mg

Taco Salad

1 pound ground round
¼ teaspoon chili powder
⅛ teaspoon cayenne pepper
¼ teaspoon cumin
1 cup diced tomatoes
⅛ teaspoon hot sauce
1 cup diced onion
Shredded lettuce
½ cup reduced-fat Monterey
    Jack cheese, shredded

Mix ground beef with chili powder, cayenne, and cumin. In nonstick pan, brown ground beef mixture. Remove from heat; drain fat. Stir in tomatoes, hot sauce, and onion. Arrange lettuce in serving dish; top with ground beef and shredded cheese. Serve with oil-free tortilla chips.

Yield: 6 servings

Nutrients per serving:

Calories 218 Fat 7 g Carbohydrate 6 g Protein 32 g Sodium 146 mg Cholesterol 81 mg

Light 'n' Spicy Beef Strips

1 pound round steak
¾ cup mild soy sauce
½ teaspoon ginger
1 clove garlic, minced
Fresh or frozen mixed
   vegetables (optional)

Cut steak into thin strips. Combine soy sauce, ginger, and garlic in a large bowl. Add steak, and mix well. Cover and refrigerate one hour or longer.

Stir-fry beef strips and marinating liquid quickly until meat is tender. Add fresh or frozen mixed vegetables to the stir fry, if desired.

Yield: 6 servings

Nutrients per serving:

Calories 180 Fat 4 g Carbohydrate 6 g Protein 30 g Sodium 1072 mg Cholesterol 71 mg

Beans and Rice

1 cup cooked kidney beans
1 cup cooked garbanzo
   beans
1 cup cooked rice
1 cup red wine vinegar
1 teaspoon hot sauce
1 teaspoon garlic powder
1 tablespoon dry minced
   onion

Mix beans and rice together. Add vinegar, hot sauce, garlic, and onion; toss lightly. Chill before serving.

Yield: 6 servings

Nutrients per serving:

Calories 108 Fat 0 g Carbohydrate 24 g Protein 6 g Sodium 148 mg Cholesterol 0 mg

Peachy Surprise

1 (4-serving) package sugar-free fat-free instant vanilla pudding
2 cups skim milk
3 medium peaches, peeled and chopped
¼ cup raspberries

Prepare pudding with milk per package directions; stir in peaches. Spoon mixture into 6 dessert glasses; top with raspberries. Chill thoroughly before serving.

Yield: 6 servings

Nutrients per serving:
_____

Calories 65 Fat 0 g Carbohydrate 14 g Protein 5 g Sodium 197 mg Cholesterol 0 mg

Tart 'n' Tangy Punch

3 cups orange juice
½ cup lemon juice
2 cups ginger ale
1 cup cranberry juice cocktail
1 cup water
Lemon slices (optional)

Combine first 5 ingredients. Chill before serving. Garnish with lemon slices, if desired.

Yield: 7½ cups

Nutrients per 1 cup:
_____

Calories 92 Fat 0 g Carbohydrate 24 g Protein 0 g Sodium 6 mg Cholesterol 0 mg

Protein foods—meat and dairy products—tend to carry more fat. Make smaller protein portions more appealing by dicing into cubes or cutting into strips and mixing in with a generous helping of vegetables.

Labor Day

Dixie Holiday

I woke to the hum of the day's first motorboat to ripple the surface of Lake Martin near Alexander City, Alabama. The cool morning breeze blew across my face as I peeked through the screen to see who could be fool enough to rise so early on a holiday that was supposed to be relaxing. I stretched and rolled over, realizing I wasn't ready to admit the sun had risen. When I opened my eyes for the second time, the patter of dog's paws on the cabin's hardwood floors and the smell of pancakes laced with fresh blueberries awakened my senses for good. Yawning, I reached for my robe and set out to claim my spot at the table.

The first batch of my uncle's specialty had already landed on the plates of my aunt, my parents, and my cousin and his friends. My new boyfriend had also pulled up a chair and was indulging in more maple syrup. Having grown up in Michigan, he wasn't quite accustomed to all this Southern hospitality. We had driven down from my parents' home in Birmingham the day before, after cheering the Crimson Tide on to victory. He would later tell me that what he remembered of his Labor Day weekend in Dixie was "football and food."

When the last dish was wiped clean, we donned our swimsuits and piled into the boat for a few hours of skiing and sightseeing. I noticed that the scenery had changed somewhat since our last Labor Day reunion at the lake. There seemed to be even less of the little island that had poked through the water so brazenly just a raft ride away from the pier. All that remained of this once oasis of land were two trees with barely a pile of sand to cling to.

Back from the boat ride, we munched on apples, cheese, and crackers and staked out corners of solitude in the pines, catching up on the latest novels and doing a little daydreaming. An early dinner of barbecued chicken, corn on the cob, fresh green beans, and apple pie sent us on our way home. But where the dirt road runs into the highway, my dad spotted some muscadine vines hanging from the trees. Only after filling our pockets with the luscious grapes were we ready to relinquish the day.

Charlotte Snow
Washington, D.C.

If your area allows them, FIREWORKS ARE ALWAYS A FUN ADDITION to a Labor Day picnic. This holiday marks the end of the summer, so let it close with a big bang.

REMEMBER IT'S A DAY OF REST AND RELAXATION, so don't spend every minute shopping for school clothing. Be lazy…do nothing for a change. It's a great weekend to catch up on reading that you have been neglecting. Park yourself in a big hammock away from everything.

LITTLE-LABOR GATHERING

Hot 'n' Spicy Ketchup
Crunchy Macaroni Salad

🐛 🐛 🐛

Picnic Onion Burgers
Tomato and Onion Salad

🐛 🐛 🐛

Peachy-Blueberry Surprise
Old-Fashioned Pink Lemonade

🐛 🐛 🐛

Hot 'n' Spicy Ketchup

½ cup ketchup
½ teaspoon onion powder
¼ teaspoon garlic powder
¼ teaspoon horseradish
¼ teaspoon hot sauce

Combine all ingredients. Mix well. Serve with hot dogs and hamburgers.

Yield: about ¾ cup

Nutrients per tablespoon:

Calories 16 Fat 0 g Carbohydrate 4 g Protein 0 g Sodium 181 mg Cholesterol 0 mg

Crunchy Macaroni Salad

2 cups cooked elbow
   macaroni
¾ cup nonfat mayonnaise
½ cup chopped onion
1 cup broccoli flowerets
¼ cup red bell pepper

Combine all ingredients. Chill before serving.

Yield: 8 servings

Nutrients per serving:

Calories 76 Fat 0 g Carbohydrate 16 g Protein 2 g Sodium 289 mg Cholesterol 0 mg

Fresh tastes best! Enjoy a healthy serving from the last of nature's summer harvest.

Picnic Onion Burgers

2 pounds ground round
   steak
2 teaspoons onion powder
½ cup finely chopped onion
2 teaspoons black pepper
2 teaspoons hot sauce
2 tablespoons chopped
   parsley

*Combine all ingredients. Mix
well. Shape into eight patties.
Broil or grill to desired doneness.*

Yield: 8 servings

Nutrients per serving:

Calories 157 Fat 4 g Carbohydrate 1 g Protein 29 g Sodium 52 mg Cholesterol 71 mg

Tomato and Onion Salad

4 cups diced tomato
2 cups diced onion
2 teaspoons black pepper
2 cups white vinegar

*Combine tomato and onion; mix
lightly. Stir black pepper into
white vinegar. Pour over vegetable mixture. Toss to mix well.
Chill before serving.*

Yield: 8 servings

Nutrients per serving:

Calories 33 Fat 0 g Carbohydrate 8 g Protein 2 g Sodium 8 mg Cholesterol 0 mg

Peachy-Blueberry Surprise

6 medium peaches, sliced
2 cups blueberries
¼ cup light brown sugar
2 teaspoons cinnamon
1 cup rolled oats

Preheat oven to 350°. Combine peaches and blueberries in a baking dish. Mix brown sugar, cinnamon, and oats together. Sprinkle oat mixture over fruit. Heat for about 20 minutes, or until topping has toasted and fruit is tender.

Yield: 8 servings

Nutrients per serving:

Calories 111 Fat 0 g Carbohydrate 27 g Protein 2 g Sodium 0 g Cholesterol 0 mg

Old-Fashioned Pink Lemonade

1½ cups lemon juice
2 quarts water
½ cup cherry juice
Sugar or sweetener to taste

Combine all ingredients. Serve over ice. Sweeten to taste, if desired.

Yield: 10 cups

Nutrients per (1-cup) serving:

Calories 8 Fat 0 g Carbohydrate 2 g Protein 0 g Sodium 0 mg Cholesterol 0 mg

Tailgating

Prelude to the Game

The Grove is the pastoral site on the Ole Miss campus in Oxford, Mississippi, where the faithful gather to celebrate Rebel football and perpetuate tradition. Tailgating reaches its ultimate in the Grove, and there are as many ways to do it as there are Ole Miss fans.

There are many who go formal with candelabra, china, and crystal. Not me. My tailgate technique developed as a result of my preference for hob-nobbing and chit-chatting over set-up and clean-up. The more simple and swift the assembly of the feast, the more time for enjoying the students and friends surrounding the tables. The most important ingredient to expedient service and clearance is a collection of plastic storage bins ranging in size from blanket box to margarine tub. These handy fellows lend themselves to speedy display—simply remove the lid, and place it under the container—and easy game-time storage—replace the lid and, if necessary, return to ice chest. When the party is over, the able-bodied seem to disappear rapidly, so the packing away is easy. I dedicate the dining room to my Grove Goodies during the football season and replace and keep the non-perishables packed there in readiness for the game. We have a 6-foot table of the institutional variety that takes two men to carry but will survive for generations. It and the "bar" cardtable and 10 folding chairs live in the back of the family Suburban from August through November. With six trips to Oxford on schedule, we don't load and unload on a weekly basis. The latest addition to my tailgate collection is a catering-size chafing dish. I pined for it until my husband relented. Some women crave jewels and furs—I go for stainless steel and sterno! Now we can add barbecue and grilled chicken breasts to our repertoire of edible offerings.

I have some old reliable food items that make every trip: fried chicken, roasted peanuts, deli meat on rolls with homemade mayonnaise, strawberries and powdered sugar, apple slices and caramel dip. The main secret to successful Grove food is ease of consumption. If it takes much effort to put together or to eat, you will be taking it home. Paper plates and napkins make the trip every time so they live in the big blanket box with the Zip-Lock bags. Trash bags are indispensable, as is a large cooler filled for use as an ice bucket bar-side.

Few folks are quite as obsessive as I am, but almost any of the tailgate techniques will stand alone without the whole performance. If you have a favorite team—Cheers! If not, Ole Miss is willing to be adopted, and you won't be disappointed even if the team isn't victorious. Hoddy-Toddy!

Ruth Summers
Memphis, Tn

211

A HANDY ITEM IS A LARGE, STURDY LAUNDRY BASKET for hauling such essentials as bottled libations and mixers.

 A CENTERPIECE SUGGESTION consists of a tall, heavy (the wind can be a factor) florist's vase stuffed with pom-poms and your college flags. A statue of your mascot is the essential final touch.

 FOR THE BAR, a small basket containing jiggers, iced tea spoons, napkins, salt and pepper, celery sticks, and lemon slices works well.

 After struggling with cloth table covers and post-game laundry two or three times, Ruth made a trip to the local fabric shop and purchased SEVERAL YARDS OF FLANNEL-BACKED VINYL in the traditional school colors. Not only is this material colorful, it can also be hung over the volleyball net when you get home, hosed off, and air-dried; no ironing is required.

 A MOBILE PHONE is a must to take to a game to gather all your friends to one spot.

 Check at your local party supply store for face painting supplies, and TREAT THE GANG TO MASCOTS OR SCHOOL COLORS PAINTED ON THEIR CHEEKS. This pre-game activity will get everyone in the spirit for the kickoff.

THREE CHEERS FOR LUNCH

Temptin' Time-Out Bread Snack
Summer-Style Macaroni and Cheese

🦌 🦌 🦌

Vegetable Beef Shish Kebab
Marinated Eggplant

🦌 🦌 🦌

Orange Bowls
Lemon Fizz

🦌 🦌 🦌

Temptin' Time-Out Bread Snack

3 tablespoons cider vinegar
1 tablespoon olive oil
½ teaspoon garlic powder
3 medium tomatoes, chopped
1 tablespoon oregano
12 mini bread loaf slices

Mix vinegar, olive oil, and garlic powder together; set aside. Toss tomatoes with oregano. Pour vinegar oil mixture over tomatoes. Crispen bread slices in a warm oven; then top each slice with approximately 1 tablespoon of tomato mixture.

Yield: 4 to 6 servings

Nutrients per slice:

Calories 24 Fat 1 g Carbohydrate 3 g Protein 0 g Sodium 10 mg Cholesterol 0 mg

Summer-Style Macaroni and Cheese

2 cups cooked elbow macaroni
¼ cup shredded reduced fat Cheddar cheese
¼ cup sliced green onion
½ cup chopped red bell pepper
¼ cup red wine vinegar

Combine macaroni, cheese, and vegetables. Add vinegar; toss lightly. Chill before serving.

Yield: 6 servings

Nutrients per serving:

Calories 129 Fat 3 g Carbohydrate 15 g Protein 8 g Sodium 135 mg Cholesterol 13 mg

Vegetable Beef Shish Kebab

2 onions, cut into chunks
2 green peppers, cut into chunks
1 cup mushroom halves
2 tomatoes, cut into chunks
1 pound top round steak, cubed
½ cup barbecue sauce

Cook vegetables in vegetable steamer for 1 minute. On four individual skewers, alternate steak and vegetables. Grill over hot charcoal, brushing with barbecue sauce while cooking.

Yield: 4 servings

Nutrients per serving:

Calories 226 Fat 5 g Carbohydrate 19 g Protein 31 g Sodium 318 mg Cholesterol 71 mg

Marinated Eggplant

1 large eggplant
1 cup nonfat Italian dressing
1 teaspoon rosemary
¼ teaspoon oregano
½ teaspoon black pepper

Peel eggplant; cut into ½-inch slices. Mix dressing with rosemary, oregano, and black pepper, and pour over eggplant slices in shallow dish. Allow to marinate one hour or longer. Marinated eggplant can be broiled, grilled, or steamed.

Yield: 4 servings

Nutrients per serving:

Calories 29 Fat 0 g Carbohydrate 6 g Protein 0 g Sodium 580 mg Cholesterol 0 mg

Orange Bowls

6 large oranges
1 cup red grapes, coarsely
 chopped
½ cup pineapple tidbits

Cut off tops of oranges; remove fruit from skin, leaving shells intact. Chop orange sections into small chunks and combine with grapes and pineapple. Spoon fruit mixture into orange shells.

Yield: 6 servings

Nutrients per serving:

Calories 97 Fat 0 g Carbohydrate 26 g Protein 1 g Sodium 1 mg Cholesterol 0 mg

Lemon Fizz

¾ cup lemon juice
 Powdered sugar substitute
 (equal to ½ cup powdered
 sugar)
1 quart water
2 cups sugar-free ginger ale

Mix lemon juice and powdered sugar substitute together. Add water and ginger ale; stir well. Serve over ice.

Yield: 6 (1-cup) servings

Nutrients per serving

Calories 40 Fat 0 g Carbohydrate 10 g Protein 0 g Sodium 0 mg Cholesterol 0 mg

Lighter meal planning is easy if you organize around the starchy foods—potatoes, corn, rice, pasta—then add meat and cheese as flavorful condiments.

Index

a

222

Festive Fare

Wimmer Cookbook Distribution
4210 B. F. Goodrich Blvd.
Memphis, TN 38118

Please send _____ copies of **Festive Fare** @ $15.95 each _____
Tennessee residents add sales tax @ $1.32 each _____
Postage and handling @ $5.00 each _____
TOTAL _____

Charge to Visa ( ) or MasterCard ( ) # _____

Exp. Date _____

Signature _____

Name _____

Address _____

City _____ State _____ Zip _____

- -

Cookbook Lovers Take Note. . .
. . . .

If you've enjoyed **Festive Fare**, The Wimmer Companies, Inc., has a catalog of 250 other cookbook titles that may interest you. To receive your free copy, write:

The Wimmer Companies, Inc.
4210 B. F. Goodrich Blvd.
Memphis, TN 38118

Or call 1-800-727-1034